The Philosophy of *Qi*

Translations from the Asian Classics

A portrait of Kaibara Ekken at age sixty-five, said to have been painted by the Kyoto artist Kano Shren.

The Philosophy of *Qi*
The *Record of Great Doubts*

KAIBARA EKKEN

TRANSLATED, WITH AN INTRODUCTION, BY
MARY EVELYN TUCKER

COLUMBIA UNIVERSITY PRESS   NEW YORK

*Columbia University Press wishes to express its
appreciation for assistance given by the Thomas Berry
Foundation toward the cost of publishing this book.*

Columbia University Press
Publishers Since 1893
New York   Chichester, West Sussex

Library of Congress Cataloging-in-Publication Data
Kaibara, Ekken, 1630–1714.
   [Taigiroku. English]
   The Philosophy of qi: the record of great doubts /
Kaibara Ekken ; translated, with an introduction, by
Mary Evelyn Tucker.
         p. cm. — (Translations from the Asian
classics)
   Includes bibliographical references and index.
   ISBN 0-231-13922-5 (alk. paper)
   ISBN 0-231-51129-9 (electronic)
1. Conduct of life—Early works to 1800. I. Tucker,
Mary Evelyn. II. Title. III. Series.

B5244.K253T3513 2007
181'.12—dc22

                              2006025278

To my parents,
Mary Elizabeth Hayes Tucker and William Duane Tucker, Jr.,
who supported me on the path of doubt and discovery

ACKNOWLEDGMENTS

This work has unfolded over two decades with the help of many people, to whom I am deeply grateful.

Among them are my teachers at Columbia University, Wm. Theodore de Bary, Wing-tsit Chan, and Irene Bloom, who set the standard for translations and commentaries that has shaped the field of Neo-Confucian studies. Their dedicated efforts to make the Neo-Confucian tradition understood and appreciated in the West have been unparalleled. Contributing significantly to these efforts has been the Confucian scholar Tu Weiming, Director of the Harvard Yenching Institute. Their comprehensive interpretive framework of Confucian humanism has influenced hundreds of students and scholars on both sides of the Pacific. Moreover, the tireless dedication of Ted de Bary and Tu Weiming as engaged intellectuals interpreting Confucianism and the challenges of modernity has been an inspiration to me and to countless others. Steadily behind so much of this work is Fanny de Bary.

I am also indebted to the Japanese scholars Okada Takehiko and Minamoto Ryōen for their many years of encouragement of my study of Kaibara Ekken. Professor Okada welcomed me to his home on several occasions and provided me with copies of original documents of Ekken's writings. Watanabe Kimie accompanied me to visit Professor Okada, and her support of this work has meant more than I can say. She and her husband, Tatsuhiko, provided me with the woodblock prints of birds, fish, shells, leaves, and flowers from a nineteenth-century edition of Ekken's *Plants of Japan* (*Yamato honzō*) that illustrate this book.

For answering questions regarding the translation, I am deeply grateful to Noriko Narita, Takako Noguchi, and Ron Guey Chu, whose generous assistance to so many can never be repaid.

In providing helpful evaluations of the manuscript to Columbia University Press, I am grateful to Janine Sawada, John Berthrong, John Tucker, and Tu Weiming. In assisting with pinyin romanization and preparation of the glossary, I am indebted to Deborah Sommers. Michael Ashby did a superb editing job, and Columbia's staff has been most helpful, especially Jennifer Crewe, Juree Sondker, and Irene Pavitt.

Over many years, I have been grateful for the excellent secretarial assistance of Stephanie Snyder at Bucknell University and indispensable help from Ann Keeler Evans and Donna Rosenberg.

Thanks to Irene Bloom's study of Luo Qinshun in China and Young-chan Ro's book on Yi Yulgok in Korea, I was able to situate my work on Ekken's monism of *qi* in Japan in a historical lineage across East Asia. I am grateful to them and to colleagues in Japanese studies who have done path-breaking work on the Tokugawa period. These include Robert Bellah, Harold Bolitho, David Dilworth, Olof Lidin, Tetsuo Najita, Peter Nosco, Herman Ooms, Janine Sawada, and John Tucker. I have valued my conversations with Michael Kalton regarding Korean Confucianism and its contemporary relevance.

I would like to acknowledge with gratitude support from the Japan Foundation and the National Endowment for the Humanities to do the initial translation and the following foundations for their support in completing this work: V. Kann Rasmussen, Germeshausen, and Kendeda. Martin S. Kaplan and Nancy Klavans continue to be indispensable colleagues and invaluable companions in the journey toward a sustainable future.

Some of the ideas in this book were presented at conferences in Japan, Singapore, and Taiwan as well as at seminars at Columbia, Harvard, and Berkeley. I appreciated the comments and questions I received on those occasions.

Thomas Berry, John Grim, and Brian Swimme have provided incalculable moral support for this project. Their friendship over the years is a source of constant joy to me in the spirit of *qi*.

The Philosophy of *Qi*

The statue of Kaibara Ekken on his tomb at Kinryuji, a temple in the city of Fukuoka, in Kyushu.

Ekken's Life and Thought

Kaibara Ekken (1630–1714) was one of the leading Neo-Confucian thinkers of early modern Japan. Born in the beginning of the Tokugawa era (1600–1863), he had a significant intellectual influence during the period and is well respected in his birthplace of Fukuoka in northern Kyushu down to the present.[1] Ekken was raised in a lower-ranking samurai family, was sent to study in Kyoto by the local provincial government (*han*), and subsequently was employed by the provincial lord (daimyo) as a government adviser. This ensured his career as a scholar and writer relatively free from financial concerns. His remarkable productivity was, no doubt, due to his moderate but secure income, as well as to the peaceful conditions established by the unification of the country under the Tokugawa shogunate. Moreover, he received invaluable assistance from his nephew, Kaibara Chiken, and his disciple Takeda Shun'an. In addition, his wife was a talented woman who, it is conjectured, collaborated with him in some of his writings, particularly his diaries and travel accounts. Ekken was not unaware of these fortunate circumstances supporting his scholarly life. He frequently spoke of a feeling of gratitude for blessings received and the need to repay one's debt to the human and natural forces that sustain a person's life.

Ekken's sense of gratitude was closely linked to his empathic understanding of the suffering dimension of life, as he lost both his mother and his stepmother at an early age. Ekken's sympathies toward the more difficult aspects of life were, no doubt, also nurtured by growing up primarily amid townspeople outside the castle of the ruling daimyo rather than only among the samurai class. Furthermore, he lived for several of his early years in the countryside, where his proximity to the daily life of farmers inevitably stimulated his later interest in agriculture and botany. This breadth of life experience is reflected in the wide range of his concerns in his lecturing, research, and writing.

These early experiences were expanded by his later studies in Kyoto and his frequent opportunities to travel. For seven years he studied in Kyoto, the intellectual capital of his time. There he met many of the most illustrious Confucian scholars of Japan, including Kinoshita Jun'an (1621–1698), Yamazaki Ansai (1618–1682), and Itō Jinsai (1627–1705). He maintained contact with several of these scholars and paid them visits on his return trips to Kyoto. He also traveled on various occasions to the political capital, Edo (Tokyo), where he met one of the leading government advisers, the Confucian scholar Hayashi Gahō (1618–1680). In addition, he frequently visited the port city of Nagasaki in Kyushu, where he could purchase Chinese books and occasionally even Western ones. It was there at age twenty-one that he obtained a copy of the Song Neo-Confucian scholar Zhu Xi's (1130–1200) most important work, *Reflections on Things at Hand* (*Jinsilu*). Seventeen years later, he wrote the first Japanese commentary on this text, *Notes on Reflections on Things at Hand* (*Kinshiroku bikō*). This marked a significant moment in the introduction of Neo-Confucian thought into the Japanese context. It

also signaled Ekken's enormous appreciation for Zhu Xi's comprehensive Neo-Confucian synthesis.

Ekken's lifelong preoccupation with Zhu became an impetus for
introducing Confucian ideas and ethics into Japanese society, politics, and education. Ekken's breadth of concerns and understanding
regarding Confucian thought reflects his life experience, his opportunities for travel, and his contacts with scholars and other classes
in society. Impressive in Ekken's writings is not only the range and
volume of his production, but also the sincerity and humility of his
own voice. From high-level Confucian scholarship to popular treatises on Confucian morality, and from botanical and agricultural
studies to provincial topographies and genealogies, Ekken demonstrated a commitment to intellectual and ethical concerns rarely
surpassed in the Tokugawa period.

In terms of Confucian scholarship, in addition to his appreciative
commentary on Zhu Xi's *Reflections on Things at Hand*, Ekken's
most important philosophical work, the *Record of Great Doubts* (*Taigiroku*), sets forth his disagreements with Zhu Xi.[2] These two texts
illustrate the extent of both affirmation and dissent Ekken displayed
in his interactions with the writings of this leading Chinese Neo-
Confucian philosopher. His ability to be simultaneously appreciative and critical reflects something of the dynamic quality of the
Confucian tradition itself. As On-cho Ng and Kai-wing Chow have
suggested, "Confucianism was never a formalism of ideas frozen in
time, reified as immutable dogmas. Its very vitality, dynamism, and
existence depended on its remaking and reinventing itself."[3] Reinventing itself over many centuries, Confucianism and its later form
of Neo-Confucianism passed from China to Korea and then to Japan by means of a complex and at times contested set of texts, dialogues, and commentaries. This rich interaction of the tradition
with different cultural contexts and in response to new social and
political urgencies is especially present in Ekken's efforts to adapt
Confucianism to the Japanese context.

The reflections in the *Record of Great Doubts* of a seventeenth-century Japanese intellectual on some of the key philosophical ideas of a twelfth-century synthesizer of Neo-Confucianism illustrate the intellectual vitality of the Confucian tradition; a gap of five centuries did not lessen the importance of the arguments related to how one lived one's life and contributed to society. In the *Record of Great Doubts*, Ekken argues for a philosophy of vitalistic naturalism as a basis for moral self-cultivation and for active response to social and political affairs. He resists any potential tendencies in Neo-Confucian thought toward transcendental escapism, quietism, or self-centered cultivation. He aims instead to articulate a dynamic philosophy of material force (C. *qi* or *ch'i*, J. *ki*) as a unifying basis for the interaction of self, society, and nature. This philosophy is sometimes called a monism of *qi* because it posits a nondualistic integration of *li* (principle) and *qi*. In this context, self-cultivation becomes a primary means for an integrated life. Ekken emphasizes that material force as the vital spirit present in all life needs to be cultivated in oneself and enjoyed in nature.

The *Record of Great Doubts* is, then, a broad summary of Ekken's commitment to a monism of *qi*. This is the philosophical grounding for Ekken's dual interests in popularizing Confucian ethics and providing pragmatic assistance to various classes in society. Understanding principle in daily affairs was the basis for both ethics and action. His unified worldview provided a holistic and convincing basis for adopting Confucianism into Japan. In order to spread Confucian ideas among a wide variety of people, Ekken wrote moral treatises (*kunmono*) in a simplified Japanese style addressed to particular groups, including samurai, families, women, and children.[4] This was part of his profound commitment to Confucian ideas and practices as being a valuable contribution to Japanese society in its emerging period of peace and stability. For establishing a new moral social-political order, Confucianism was considered by many to be

an indispensable philosophy.[5] Ekken's writings and teachings contributed significantly to its spread and nativization in his compari-
sons of Confucianism with Shinto. As naturalistic philosophies emphasizing virtues such as authenticity and sincerity, Confucianism
and Shinto were seen by many scholars as having similar concerns.
Ekken illustrated this in his essay *Precepts on the Gods* (*Jingikun*),
where he equates the way of the Confucian sages with the way of the
Japanese gods (*kami*). He also observed that the principles of change
and constancy in nature were essential to both traditions.

The other major thrust of Ekken's thought was pragmatic and involved what has been termed practical learning (*jitsugaku*).[6] Here
Ekken's interests encompassed such areas as medicine, botany, agriculture, astronomy, geography, and mathematics. One of his best-
known works of practical learning is *Plants of Japan* (*Yamato honzō*),
a natural history of plants, herbs, shells, fish, and birds. It is based
on the long-established tradition in China of plant taxonomy. In addition, his *Precepts on Health Care* (*Yōjōkun*) is still popular in Japan.[7]
Moreover, he wrote an introduction to Miyazaki Yasusada's agricultural treatise *Nōgyō zensho*, an important explanation of farming
techniques intended to assist farmers. He also contributed to local
history and geography through his genealogies of the Kuroda *han*
and his travelogues and diaries. Ekken's diverse interests in practical learning and in investigating things in nature led him to be
called the Aristotle of Japan by a German naturalist.[8]

Underlying the clearly extraordinary range of Ekken's intellectual and moral concerns is his philosophical commitment to a vitalism expressed as a monism of *qi*, contrasting with the qualified dualism articulated by some Neo-Confucians, such as Zhu Xi, who
distinguished between principle and material force. Hence the significance of Ekken's *Record of Great Doubts*, which explains his
reservations and commitments in subtle detail. This work constitutes a central philosophical text in the history of Japanese Neo-

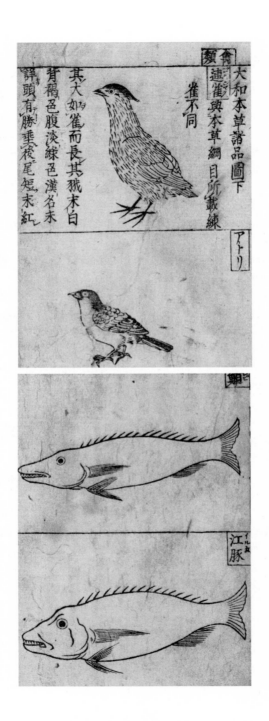

大和本草諸品圖下

禽

類 迅雀 與本草綱目所載練

雀不同

其大如雀而長其獵末白

背褐色腹淡綠色漢名未

譯頭有勝垂後尾短末紅

アトリ

ヒ

江豚

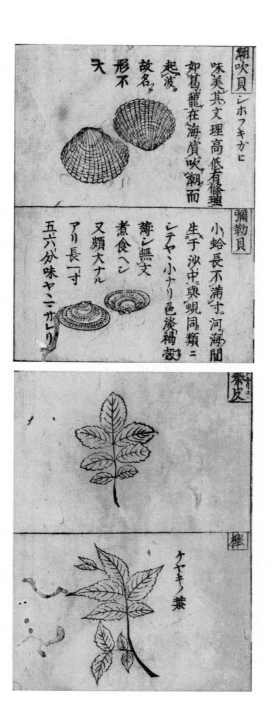

潮吹貝：レホフキガヒ

味美。其文理高低有條理
如葛籠。在海濱吹潮而
起波。
故名ヅ
形不
大

彌勒貝

小蛤長不滿寸。河海間
生于沙中。與蜆同類ニ
シテヤ、小ナリ。色淡褐殼
薄シ無文
煮食ヘシ
又頗大ナル
アリ長一寸
五六分味ヤ、カカレリ

棗皮

欅

ケヤキノ葉

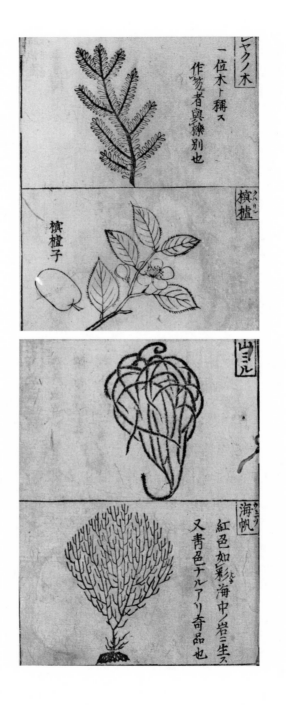

シャクノ木

一位木ト稱ス
作笏者與櫟別也

槟櫨

槟櫨子

山ミル

海帆

紅色如彩海中ノ岩ニ生ス
又青色ナルアリ奇品也

Confucianism, and for this reason warrants discussion, explication, and interpretation. The translation that follows is made available with the hope that by situating it within its East Asian philosophical lineage and its Japanese historical context, it will provoke further discussion regarding the formulation of cosmology and ethics in the Tokugawa period.[9]

The Text in the Context of East Asian Confucianism

Confucianism has been the primary vehicle for the transmission of humanistic learning and moral values in East Asia. Its imprint has been considerable not only in China but in Korea, Japan, and Vietnam as well. Indeed, it is important to note the great variety of scholars, texts, and schools that the term "Confucianism" embraces over time and across cultures. Thus it may be helpful to sketch briefly the development of Confucianism itself so as to locate the text within its larger East Asian philosophical and religious context.

Confucianism refers most basically to the thought of Confucius (Kong Qiu, 551–479 B.C.E.) and his followers in China, especially Mencius (385?–312? B.C.E.) and Xunzi (307–219? B.C.E.). This classical period (ca. 551–223 B.C.E.) of remarkable intellectual flourishing is frequently called the period of the hundred philosophers. Born in a time of rapid social change, Confucius devoted his life to reestablishing order through rectification of the individual and the state. This involved a creative transmission of earlier Chinese traditions embracing moral, political, and religious components. The texts of the early Confucian tradition are known as the Five Classics: the *Classics of History, Poetry, Changes,* and *Rites,* and the *Spring and Autumn Annals.*

The principal teachings of Confucius, as contained in the *Analects,* emphasize the practice of moral virtues, especially humaneness or love (*ren*) and filiality (*xiao*). These were exemplified by the "noble person" (*junzi*) particularly in the five relations: between parent and child, ruler and minister, husband and wife, older and younger siblings, and friend and friend. From the time of the Han dynasty (202 B.C.E.–226 C.E.), these basic Confucian ideals and their larger cosmological implications played a pivotal role in Chinese thought and institutions. Indeed, the main purpose of Han Confucianism was to elucidate the interrelations of the natural, social, and political orders so that both ruler and individuals could be effective moral agents. Heaven, Earth, and humans were seen as part of a dynamic system; by participating in this system, humans fulfilled their role in this trinity and assisted in "the transforming and nourishing process of Heaven and Earth."[10] The Han thinkers, especially Dong Zhongshu (195?–105? B.C.E.), established the philosophical and political basis for State Confucianism that was invoked by later dynasties for their own ideological ends. Confucianism was, however, somewhat eclipsed by the spread of Buddhism during the Six Dynasties (222–589), Sui (589–618), and Tang (618–960) periods.

Confucianism was revitalized in the eleventh and twelfth centuries during the Song dynasty largely by the ideas of Zhou Dunyi (1017–1073), Zhang Zai (1020–1077), Cheng Hao (1032–1085), Cheng Yi (1033–1107), and Zhu Xi (1130–1200). It was Zhu's synthesis of these thinkers and his codification of texts into the Four Books that became known as Neo-Confucianism. The Four Books, which he felt contained the central ideas of Confucian thought, are the *Analects*, *Mencius*, and two chapters of the *Record of Rites*: the *Great Learning* and the *Doctrine of the Mean*. These texts and Zhu's commentaries on them became the basis for the civil service examination system that endured in China for some six hundred years. With this system, government officials were selected for office on the basis of Confucian moral education. Confucianism thus became the foundation for a meritocracy in contrast to the achievement of office by privilege, rank, or birth.

Zhu's *Reflections on Things at Hand* is a central Neo-Confucian text. This anthology of Song Neo-Confucian thought is considered to be "unquestionably the most important single work of philosophy produced in the Far East during the second millennium A.D."[11] Zhu himself describes the work in the following manner: "The Four Books are the ladders to the Six Classics, the *Jinsilu* is the ladder to the Four Books."[12]

In this work, Zhu compiled texts that provided, for the first time, a comprehensive metaphysical basis for Confucian thought and practice. In response to the Buddhists' metaphysics of emptiness and their perceived tendency toward withdrawal from the world in meditative practices, Zhu formulated a spirituality based on a balance of religious reverence, ethical practice, scholarly investigation, and political participation. The disillusionment caused by the failure of political reforms in the Northern Song dynasty led Zhu Xi to advocate the moral and spiritual education of individuals in order to affect the larger social and political order. He outlined a program of study that was broadly and practically based and yet had a deep regard for the unique moral and spiritual cultivation of each person. To investigate things without and to have reverence within were the two complements of his thought.

Unlike the Buddhists, who saw human ignorance of the impermanent nature of the world as a source of suffering, Zhu Xi, and the Neo-Confucians after him, affirmed change as the source of transformation in both the cosmos and the person. Thus Neo-Confucian spiritual discipline involved cultivating one's moral nature so as to bring it into harmony with the larger pattern of change in the cosmos. Moral virtues were often paired with a cosmological counterpart; the central virtue of humaneness (C. *ren*, J. *jin*), for example, was seen as the source of fecundity and growth in both the individual and the cosmos (C. *yuan*, J. *gen*). By practicing humaneness, one could effect the transformation of things in oneself, in society, and in the cosmos. In so doing, one realized a deeper identity with reality, characterized as "forming one body with all things" (C. *wan wu yi ti*, J. *banbutsu ittai*). This process of cultivation involved disciplining one's mind and heart, which is represented by a single character in Chinese (*shin*) and Japanese (*kokoro*). Thus the mental and emotional dimensions of humans are intertwined and are translated here as mind-and-heart.

Confucian thought, political institutions, social organization, and educational curricula had a profound influence on China, Korea, and Vietnam. Chinese influence in Vietnam, felt as early as the Han dynasty, was long lasting; indeed, northern Vietnam was a part of the Chinese empire for a millennium (111 B.C.E.–993 C.E.). Confucian thought passed into Korea beginning in the third and fourth centuries, and into Japan in the sixth and seventh centuries; it has had a lasting impact on the social, political, and educational systems of both countries. As in China, in Korea, too, Zhu Xi's commentaries on the Four Books became the foundation for the civil service examination system. This system of selecting government officials on the basis of merit rather than hereditary privilege lasted in China and Korea until the early twentieth century. In Japan, although there were no civil service examinations, the Four Books and Zhu's commentaries became the basis of the samurai educational curriculum in the premodern period. These texts were particularly important during the Tokugawa period, when Confucianism spread through schools and through the writings and lectures of individual scholars such as Ekken.

Zhu Xi's influence on East Asian thought and education has clearly been significant and enduring. In this context, a work such as Ekken's *Record of Great Doubts* takes on particular importance. Ekken provided the Japanese not only with the first accessible commentary on Zhu Xi's *Reflections on Things at Hand* but also with one of the first fully developed disagreements with Zhu. Thus both affirmation and dissent are represented in Ekken's work as he developed his own articulation of the philosophy of material force.

Material Force (*Qi*)

Wing-tsit Chan has translated *qi* as "material force," something that consists of both matter and energy.[13] Chan notes that before the notion of *li* developed in the Neo-Confucian tradition, *qi* referred to the "psychophysiological power associated with blood and breath."[14] He also suggests that the words "matter" or "ether" are not adequate translations for *qi* because they convey only one aspect of the term.[15]

One of the earliest appearances of the term *qi* in the classical period is in the writings of Mencius, who refers to *qi* as "that which fills the body."[16] In this context, *qi* can be translated as "vital force" or "vital power."[17] Mencius notes that the *qi* that fills one's body is directed by the will. He observes that it is important not to abuse or block one's *qi* but to allow it to flow freely. If one does this and nourishes one's *qi*, it will fill the space between Heaven and Earth. A famous reference in *Mencius* speaks of a "flood-like *qi*," sometimes translated as a "strong, moving power."[18] Mencius says that this floodlike *qi* is difficult to explain. He comments, nonetheless, on the importance of nourishing it, for, he says, that *qi* is,

> in the highest degree, vast and unyielding. Nourish it with integrity and place no obstacle in its path and it will fill the space between Heaven and Earth. It is a *qi* which unites rightness and the Way. Deprive it of these and it will collapse. It is born of accumulated rightness and cannot be appropriated by anyone through a sporadic show of rightness. Whenever one acts in a way that falls below the standard set in one's heart, it will collapse.[19]

It is clear that this psychophysical energy must be cultivated carefully, for it is what links us to all other living things. In other words, in humans *qi* is a special form of material energy that can be nurtured through self-cultivation, which contributes to our moral and physical well-being and provides a basis for respecting other humans. The whole universe is, likewise, filled with the matter-energy of *qi*. By nourishing not only our own *qi* but also the consciousness of our connection to this energy in nature we become full participants in the dynamic, transformative processes of the universe. That is because *qi* is the underlying unity of life, simultaneously moral and physical, spiritual and material. These ideas are further developed by Zhang Zai, Zhu Xi, and Luo Qinshun in China and such other Neo-Confucians as Yi Yulgok in Korea and Kaibara Ekken in Japan.

Zhang Zai's Development of the Concept of Material Force

Zhang Zaï's (1020–1077) great contribution to Neo-Confucian thought was his elaboration of *qi* as the vital material force that runs throughout creation. *Qi* is in a constant process of transformation that is self-generating. This change, however, is not simply random, illusory, or purposeless. Underlying the dynamic movement of *qi* is the pattern of the alternation of yin and yang. Thus all change, he asserts, occurs by means of principles (*li*). These principles or patterns of change are not simply repetitious or static entities. Each event, thing, or person is unique and hence of moral value in the continually unfolding process of *qi*: "In what has been created through stages of formation and transformation, no single thing (in the universe) is exactly like another."[20] The constantly changing quality of *qi*, then, is its dynamic force, which reveals both pattern and uniqueness as inherent in the universe.

Zhang Zai took an important step for Neo-Confucian metaphysics when he identified *qi* with the void, or the Great Vacuity (*taixu*). The distinguished twentieth-century Neo-Confucian scholar Tang

Junyi (1909–1978) saw this as an attempt to synthesize the notion of *qi* as understood by the scholars of the Jin and the Han with the emptiness of the Daoists and the Buddhists.[21] This synthesis contains two significant aspects, which Tang characterized as the vertical aspect and the horizontal aspect. In its vertical aspect, Zhang essentially provided a basis for asserting the unity of being and nonbeing, thus challenging the Buddhist and Daoist positions, which gave priority to emptiness and nonbeing respectively. In its horizontal aspect, Zhang provided a metaphysical explanation for intercommunion and change in the phenomenal world by means of the voidness of *qi*. Both the vertical and horizontal dimensions laid the groundwork for Zhang's theory of mind as having a cosmic basis. Essentially he aimed to show the intrinsic connection between the human mind and the cosmic order by means of a shared *qi*. Thus humans have the potential for understanding the underlying unity of *qi* behind all forms of change. Furthermore, humans have the capacity for intersubjective empathy with all of creation through comprehending the constant fusion and diffusion of *qi*. Zhang set forth these ideas in the *Western Inscription* (*Ximing*), where he indicates metaphorically that humans are the children of Heaven and Earth.

The Vertical Aspect of Zhang Zai's Synthesis: Metaphysical Position

In developing the concept of *qi*, Zhang Zai, like other Confucians before him, drew on the *Classic of Changes* as one of his chief sources of inspiration. His cosmology is distinctive, however, in that he identifies *qi* with the unity of all life. He describes the two aspects of *qi* as its substance (*ti*) and its function (*yong*). As substance it is known as the Great Vacuity, the primal undifferentiated material force, while as function it is the Great Harmony (*taihe*), the continuous process of integration and disintegration. The significance of differentiating these dual aspects of *qi* is its affirmation of the underlying unity of being and nonbeing, of the seen and the unseen. Thus both inner spirit and external transformation are understood as part of a whole, which is the constant appearance and disappearance of *qi*. Comprehending this reality brings one to "penetrate the secret of change,"[22] the understanding that material force is never destroyed, only transformed. While the forms of things are constantly changing, there is nonetheless a "constant unity of being and nonbeing."[23]

The significance of Zhang's metaphysical position is that it provided a comprehensive explanation of change that could then be related to the process of spiritual growth and cultivation in human beings. Change is affirmed as purposive and humans are called upon to identify with change and participate in the transformation of things.

Zhang Zai emphasizes his position in contrast to the Daoist belief that being arises from nonbeing and in contrast to the Buddhist tendency to emphasize the illusory quality of reality. He wanted neither to transcend change, as he suggested Buddhists aimed to do in meditation, nor to prolong life, as the Daoists tried to do with elixirs and practices to nurture the body.[24] Instead, he affirms the phenomenal world as a manifestation of *qi*. Moreover, he does not see nonbeing as a void into which phenomena disappear and are annihilated. Rather, he sees it in more positive terms as the source not only of life but also of generation and transformation; material force transforms through "fusion and intermingling."[25] He writes that "the integration and disintegration of material force is to the Great Vacuity as the freezing and melting of ice is to water. If we realize that the Great Vacuity is identical with material force, we know that there is no such thing as non-being."[26] Thus the Great Vacuity is the unmanifested aspect of the creativity and fecundity of the universe. The Great Harmony is its manifested aspect. They are not two separate things.

Ultimately Zhang Zai's identification of *qi* with the Great Vacuity intended to overcome any duality between that which produces and that which is produced, between substance and function. "If one says that the Great Vacuity can produce *qi* (i.e., is itself distinct from *qi*) then," he writes, "this means that the Void is infinite whereas *qi* is finite, and that the noumenal (*ti*) is distinct from the phenomenal (*yong*). This leads . . . to . . . failure to understand the constant principle of unity between being and non-being."[27] Apprehension of this essential unity is what Tang Junyi calls the vertical aspect of Zhang Zai's identification of *qi* with the void.

The Horizontal Aspect of Zhang Zai's Synthesis: Ethical Implications

The horizontal aspect, according to Tang, is the voidness of *qi* itself, which accounts for the constant intercourse and, hence, generation of things. Transformation depends on the interpenetration and "mutual prehension"[28] of things. They could not occur unless the *qi* of all things was empty, for the emptiness becomes the matrix of intersubjectivity. Thus things and persons can become uniquely present to one another through the mutual resonance of the voidness of *qi*. As Tang writes, "whenever a thing is in intercourse with another it is always that the thing by means of its void contains the other and prehends it."[29] Spatiality or emptiness is the means by which communion occurs and hence change becomes possible. Generation and transformation arise because through the void things can "diffuse their ether (*qi*) and extend themselves to other objects."[30] This fusion and diffusion of *qi* is expressed by Zhang Zai as extension (*shen*) and transformation (*hua*). Through these two principles of change, material force has the power both to produce and to be produced. Creativity and communion are possible, then, by the very nature of material force itself.

The whole universe can be seen as in a process of generation and evolution, which are themselves regarded as positive qualities exhibiting moral characteristics.[31] Zhang expresses this as follows:

> Spirituality or extension is the virtue of Heaven
> Transformation is the way of Heaven
> Its virtue is its substance, its way its function
> Both become one in the ether (*qi*).[32]

In an analogous manner, humans have a moral nature that is exhibited in the virtues of rightness and humaneness. Rightness in humans corresponds to transformation and differentiation in the natural order, for it brings things to completion. Similarly, humaneness corresponds to generation and extension, for it means sharing the same feeling. The fecundity of the cosmological order has its counterpart in the activation of virtue in the human order. Central to Zhang Zai's cosmology is his assertion that the task of the human is to understand and identify with the transformation of things, which he sees as essentially a spiritual process. He writes, "All molds and forms are but dregs of this spiritual transformation."[33] The person who knows the principles of transformation will be able to "forward the undertakings of Heaven and Earth."[34] His comprehensive affirmation of the role of the human in the universe can be seen in the *Western Inscription*, where he identifies the human with the whole cosmic order:

> Heaven is my father, Earth is my mother and even such a small creature as I finds an intimate place in their midst.
> Therefore, that which fills the universe I regard as my body and that which directs the universe I consider as my nature.
> All people are my brothers and sisters, and all things are my companions. . . .

> In life I follow and serve [Heaven and Earth]. In death I will be
> at peace.[35]

Zhang Zai's ethical, "mystical humanism"[36] is the necessary corollary to his understanding of the dynamics of change in the physical order. He sees the same process of fusion and intermingling as acting in the human through the operation of humaneness. Change holds a great creative potential for growth and fulfillment. Yet he realizes that there is also a mystery of interaction that is impossible to grasp fully: "This is the wonder that lies in all things."[37]

For Zhang, the key to harmonizing human nature and the way of Heaven is the practice of sincerity. Sincerity and enlightenment are the two aspects of spiritual practice, of the cultivation of one's nature and the investigation of things. In this balancing of inner and outer wisdom, Zhang distinguishes between nature and destiny, saying that nature is endowed by Heaven and is not obscured by material force. Destiny he defines as what is decreed by Heaven and permeates one's nature. One of the goals of achieving sagehood is to develop one's nature and thus fulfill one's destiny. In this way, a person can form one body with all things.

The significance of these distinctions in Zhang Zai' s thought is that he maintains (in the tradition of Mencius) that human nature is originally good. To account for evil he does, however, posit two natures, an original one and a physical one. This is something Ekken did not embrace, although he follows Zhang's larger understanding of a monism of *qi*. Evil arises because of imbalances in our physical nature that, in turn, result from the mingling of our physical nature with *qi*. Material force emerges from its undifferentiated state in the Great Vacuity, and differentiation arises in its phenomenal appearances. Because of this inevitable process, conflict and opposition are bound to arise and hence also evil. He recognizes that physical nature, while not evil in itself, has the potential for giving rise to evil in human actions. It is possible, however, to recover one's original nature through moral cultivation. Indeed, one can over-come any incipient tendencies toward evil by enlarging one's mind to embrace all things through intensive study. Zhang Zai notes that "the great benefit of learning is to enable oneself to transform his own physical nature."[38] Zhang also observes that the mind can har-monize human nature and feelings. This doctrine of the mind, however, is left for later Neo-Confucians to develop more fully.

In summary, Zhang Zai's doctrine of the Great Vacuity provides a metaphysical basis by which to explain the unity and the constant interaction and penetration of things. It also gives an ethical ground-ing for understanding the interactions among people. The agency of both the fecundity of the natural order and the activation of virtue in the human order in effecting change and transformation can be understood as possible because of spatiality and emptiness. As Wing-tsit Chan has pointed out, it is precisely this condition that al-lows all things to realize their authenticity and full being. For "only when reality is a vacuity can the material force operate and only with the operation of the material force can things mutually influence, mutually penetrate and mutually be identified."[39] Identification and communion of humans with nature and with each other is possible because of the emptiness of *qi*.

With these carefully articulated metaphysical and ethical discus-sions, Zhang Zai was the first Neo-Confucian who also argued for the essential unity of principle and material force. This unified view was central to the monism or philosophy of *qi* of Luo Qinshun in Ming China, Yi Yulgok in Yi Korea, and Kaibara Ekken in Tokugawa Japan.

The Influence of the Monism of *Qi* of Luo Qinshun

In addition to the influence of Zhang Zai's unified cosmology, Ekken is indebted to the Ming Confucian Luo Qinshun (1465–1547), who initially articulated his disagreements with Zhu's qualified dualism in his important text *Knowledge Painfully Acquired (Kunzhiji).*[40] First published in China in 1528, it was republished more than ten times in the Ming and Qing periods. It was reprinted in Korea and from there was brought to Japan after the Japanese expeditions to Korea in the 1590s. Hayashi Razan (1583–1657) was said to have read it and made a copy before 1604. A Japanese woodblock edition was issued in 1658 and read shortly afterward by Ekken, Itō Jinsai (1627–1705), Andō Seian (1622–1701), and others.[41] Similarly, in Korea, with the thought of Yi Yulgok (1536–1584), there arose another formulation of the disagreements with Zhu.[42] These thinkers, Luo, Yi, and Ekken, are the central figures in what has been termed a monism or philosophy of *qi* school of thought in East Asian Neo-Confucianism. Each wished to preserve monism over dualism with shared concerns for the relationship between cosmological perspectives and views of self-cultivation.[43]

In his work of remarkable scholarship and careful thought, Luo, following Zhang Zai, lays out his argument for the importance of *qi* as the unitary basis of reality and as the source of changes in the natural world. He argues forcefully against Zhu Xi's qualified dualism of *li* and *qi* and for the importance of the vital material force in the world. He wished to avoid either a potential transcendentalism of the Zhu Xi school of Neo-Confucianism or a subjective idealism of the Chan school of Buddhism or the Wang Yangming school of Neo-Confucianism. Instead, he emphasized viewing the world of humans as part of a single unified reality of *qi*. Acquiring knowledge of this world and of the human mind was part of the moral cultivation of the individual. Luo, like Zhang Zai, thus hoped to preserve both unity and diversity and to establish a metaphysics whereby the natural world and the human mind are identified yet distinct. These are surely perennial problems in philosophy, and the subtle deliberations of Luo had a powerful influence in the evolution of Neo-Confucian thought in China, and they also affected the development of both Korean and Japanese Neo-Confucianism. The implications for metaphysics, ethics, epistemology, and empiricism were significant, especially for promoting practical learning.

Metaphysics: Monism of *Qi*

In seeking to explain the evolution of the universe and its constant change over time, Luo speaks, in language that echoes Zhang Zai, of the unitary force of *qi*:

> That which penetrates heaven and earth and connects past and present is nothing other than material force (*qi*), which is unitary. This material force, while originally one, revolves through endless cycles of movement and tranquility, going and coming, opening and closing, rising and falling. Having become increasingly obscure, it then becomes manifest; having become manifest, it once again reverts to obscurity. It produces the warmth and coolness and the cold and heat of the four seasons, the birth, growth, gathering in, and storing of all living things, the constant moral relations of the people's daily life, the victory and defeat, gain and loss in human affairs.[44]

This *qi* has its manifestations in the seasons and in natural growth, as well as in moral relations in human life. Yet Luo insists that within this transformation and variety "there is a detailed order and an elaborate coherence which cannot ultimately be disturbed."[45] This order is principle and is, moreover, not separate from material force. Luo states repeatedly that *li* and *qi* are not different things. Indeed, he notes that he seeks a means to reconcile and recover the ultimate unity of *li* and *qi*.[46]

Material force operates throughout the universe in a process of continual disintegration and integration, like the waxing and wan-ing of yin and yang. Relying on Zhang Zai's text *Correcting Youthful Ignorance* (*Zhengmeng*), Luo describes this process:

> In its disintegrated state, *qi* is scattered and diffuse. Through integration, it forms matter, thereby giving rise to the manifold diversity of men and things. Yin and yang follow one another in endless succession, thereby establishing the great norms of heaven and earth.[47]

In another passage, Luo acknowledges the subtlety of the kind of distinctions he is trying to make in the relationship of *li* and *qi*:

> *Li* must be identified as an aspect of *qi*, and yet to identify *qi* with *li* would be incorrect. The distinction between the two is very slight, and hence it is extremely difficult to explain. Rather we must perceive it within ourselves and comprehend it in silence.[48]

Ethics: One Nature in Humans

The implications of Luo's monism is that he does not accept the distinction of two natures in humans, the original nature and physical nature posited by Zhang Zai and other Song Neo-Confucians as a means of explaining the origin of evil.

Luo maintains that in the classical Confucian tradition human nature is one. He believes that "human beings are fundamentally alike at birth in sharing the unitary *qi* and the compassionate mind."[49] Humans are united to all living things by virtue of their *qi*: "The *qi* involved in human breathing is the *qi* of the universe. Viewed from the standpoint of physical form, it is as if there were the distinction of interior and exterior, but this is actually only the coming and going of this unitary *qi*. Master Cheng said, 'Heaven (or nature) and man are basically not two. There is no need to speak of combining them.' This is also the case with *li* and *qi*."[50] He accounts for diversity by reference to Cheng Yi's phrase "Principle is one, its particularizations are diverse."[51] Luo observes: "At the inception of life when they are first endowed with *qi*, the principle of human beings and things is just one. After having attained physical form, their particularizations are diverse."[52] Along with a rejection of a dualism of an original nature and a physical nature comes a denial of an antagonism between the principles of nature and human desires. Thus human emotions and desires are affirmed as valid parts of human nature and deserving of being cultivated and expressed appropriately.

Epistemology and Empiricism: Investigating Things

In terms of knowledge, Luo's emphasis on *qi* gives rise to his strong affirmation of the importance of sense knowledge and experience. He does not see this sort of knowledge as less valid than the kind of moral knowledge derived from texts or history. He thus affirms the necessity of "investigating things" (*gewu*) and examining principles in the world as a means of acquiring knowledge. Although the idea of investigating things originated with classical Confucians in the *Great Learning*, it became a central doctrine of the school of Neo-Confucians inspired by the Cheng brothers and Zhu Xi. With Luo, however, the foundation for the extension of Confucianism into an empirical area is clearly laid, and it is precisely what happened in the thought of Kaibara Ekken in seventeenth-century Japan with his profound interest in studying the natural world.

All these ideas were adopted and adapted by Ekken in the *Record of Great Doubts*. His desire to affirm the world in its dynamic process of material force, in the feeling aspects of human nature, in the appreciation of the fecundity of the natural world, and in the investigation of things, both human and natural, was essential to Ekken's thought. His philosophy of the monism of *qi* expressed in this work formed the basis of his writings for both specialists and a broader public on Neo-Confucian ideas of cosmology and of his varied studies in aspects of practical learning—ranging from geography and history to astronomy, medicine, and mathematics.

Affirmation and Dissent: The Significance of the *Record of Great Doubts*

Like Luo Qinshun, Ekken was "a dedicated follower and a constructive critic" of Zhu Xi.[53] Ekken proposed to question respectfully yet creatively some of the principal metaphysical ideas of Zhu Xi. In so doing, he opened up the margins of dissent and called for critical reevaluation within the Neo-Confucian tradition. The *Record of Great Doubts* demonstrates the complex processes of continuity and change, adoption, and adaptation that are vital parts of an ongoing humanistic tradition such as Neo-Confucianism. As On-cho Ng and Kai-wing Chow have observed: "Both the texts and doctrines of any vital cultural tradition, such as Confucianism, are always in the midst of transformation, drift, and rupture, *in medias res*, relocated and remapped in ongoing interpretations and publications."[54] Indeed, by reconfiguring the idea of *qi*, this text illustrates that Neo-Confucianism was far from being simply a static orthodoxy passively accepted in various parts of East Asia. Rather, in a figure like Ekken and in a work such as the *Record of Great Doubts*, the intricate adaptation of a tradition through affirmation and dissent can be perceived. The text also demonstrates the painstaking efforts of Confucians to distinguish their concerns and commitments from those of the Buddhists and Daoists. They aimed above all, as Ekken makes abundantly clear, to claim involvement in—not withdrawal from—the world as a primary value.

Ekken's treatise is significant in the context of the Neo-Confucian tradition in East Asia for a number of historical, methodological, philosophical, and religious reasons.

1. Historically the text demonstrates the appeal and affirmation of Neo-Confucian ideas across cultures in East Asia. In particular, it documents the transmission and adaptation of distinctive forms of Chinese Neo-Confucianism to Japan: the monism of *qi* of Zhang Zai in the Song and Luo Qinshun in the Ming.
2. Methodologically it exemplifies the careful style of questioning and dissenting that was possible in the Neo-Confucian tradition of "learning for oneself" (*Analects* 14:25) rather than to impress others. Indeed, it affirms the importance of doubt as a method of individual inquiry for the attainment of authentic personhood and for the critical appropriation of a tradition.
3. Philosophically it argues against a separation of principle (*li*) and material force (*qi*) in favor of a monism of *qi*. Ekken suggests that the vitalistic naturalism of *qi* is preferable to the transcendental rationalism of *li* because the latter may result in quietism or withdrawal from the world. Affirmation of the world and investigation of it is indispensable to Ekken's thought.
4. Religiously it affirms the cosmological context of naturalism as a basis for Ekken's position that an individual must be in harmony with the vital material force in the universe so as to participate in the moral transformation of self and society. Thus affirming the world requires active participation in it.

The Text in the Context of Tokugawa Japan

Ekken lived during the early Tokugawa period, when Japan was emerging from the tumultuous wars and internal disruptions of the late medieval era. With the unification of Japan under the first Tokugawa shogun, Ieyasu, a new capital was established at Edo by the shogun-led government, or *bakufu*. The political and economic power of the government was solidified by Ieyasu's successors through a variety of means. Most significant were the measures taken to close the country (*sakoku*) and to attempt to control the provincial rulers (daimyo).

Observing the political and missionary encroachments of the Spanish and Portuguese in Asia in the sixteenth century, the Tokugawa *bakufu* was wary of any possible foreign interference with their power. They therefore took strong measures to prevent foreigners from entering or Japanese from leaving the country. Even Japanese who were overseas were prohibited from returning to Japan. This sealing off of the borders through the *sakoku* edicts was effective in many respects. In particular, it resulted in the suppression of Christianity and the eventual end of Japan's "Christian century," which had begun with European missionaries such as Francis Xavier, who arrived in Japan in 1549.[55] It did not, however, prevent books and other materials from entering Japan through the agency of the Dutch traders who were allowed to remain on the island of Deshima in Nagasaki harbor. Moreover, as Ronald Toby, Bob Wakabayashi, and other scholars have noted, trade with various parts of Asia was not fully suppressed.[56] Thus while Japan was closed to a foreign presence on its soil, it was not completely isolated from Chinese books and Western ideas, especially through what was known as Dutch learning.[57] Ekken himself frequently went to Nagaski to purchase books and was thus exposed to both Chinese Neo-Confucian texts and certain Western scientific texts.

The other principal means of *bakufu* control was through the political and economic administration known as the *bakuhan* system. It consisted of maintaining a seemingly delicate balance between regional autonomy (*han*) and centralized autocracy (*bakufu*). A hierarchy of political power was maintained, with the emperor in Kyoto symbolically at the apex. The shogun in Edo paid his respects to the emperor and so derived his authority from the emperor. In turn, the daimyo of each province were obligated to demonstrate their allegiance to the *bakufu* in various ways. The power of the daimyo was regulated through taxation, land distribution, and fealty obligations. Most prominent among these obligations was the system of alternate attendance in Edo known as *sankin kōtai*. The daimyo were required to travel with a large retinue to Edo every other year. There they had to maintain a residence where their wife and children lived. The cost of the travel and the residence prevented the daimyo from becoming an economic threat to the *bakufu*. Moreover, their political activities could be more closely observed by their presence in the capital. By these means, the *bakufu* maintained a strong centralized bureaucratic control in Edo.

Ekken was the beneficiary of this *bakuhan* system in various ways, primarily because it was a period of political stability after decades of warfare. He was employed for many years as an adviser to the local daimyo in Fukuoka. With this patronage came the opportunity to study in Kyoto and to travel with the *han* retinue to Edo on numerous occasions. Although the *han* asked him to do several lengthy genealogies and local histories, he also had financial support from the *han* to pursue his own interests in practical learning and in Confucian scholarship. Indeed, the benefits of his studies were felt by various classes of people in his own province and beyond.

The consequences of this time of peaceful consolidation extended also into the spheres of economics and education and encouraged the spread of Confucianism. With the decline of the samurai as a warring class, there was a need for other employment. Many of these samurai became bureaucrats or advisers to the government in Edo or in their respective provinces. Others became teachers, scholars, or tutors in the newly forming educational system under the aegis of Confucian philosophy.[58] Although there was not a civil service examination system in Japan, as there had been in China and

Korea, a new kind of literati class (*jusha*) began to emerge. The Confucian virtue of meritocracy was especially valued by this literati class as its members became leading educators and political advisers. Moreover, the moral philosophy, political theory, and practical learning of Confucianism appealed to the samurai as well as to those of other classes.

The rising intellectual influence of the samurai was somewhat offset by the growing economic power of merchants. Trade flourished along the Tōkaidō road to Edo. Osaka, in particular, became a center of bustling economic activity. Confucianism was invoked also by the merchants to articulate the educational philosophy of their Osaka academy, known as the Kaitokudō.[59] Even the farmers benefited, from the publication of agricultural manuals stimulated by the practical learning concerns of Confucian scholars such as Ekken.

The Spread of Confucian Ideas and Values

The relative peace and growing prosperity of the early Tokugawa period were ideal conditions for the gradual spread of Confucianism to many strata of the closed society. The reasons for this growth are manifold and deserving of further exploration. At a minimum, however, it is worth noting that not least of these reasons was the inherent appeal of Confucianism itself.[60] With Ekken this appeal is evident in his ardent embrace of Confucian moral thought and in his drive to spread Confucian ideas to diverse classes of society. Through his work and that of others, Confucian values were disseminated through various levels of society. This dissemination was made possible by the rapid growth of inexpensive printing methods and the increased literacy due to the establishment of schools. Tetsuo Najita has described the diffusion of Confucianism in Tokugawa Japan:

> The importance of Confucianism as a source from which key mediating concepts were drawn to grapple with specific moral issues

confronting Tokugawa commoners is easily confirmed by the available literature of the period. In the case of merchants, Confucianism offered a language with which to conceptualize their intellectual worth in terms of universalistic definitions of "virtue." Thus while Confucianism undeniably remained the preferred philosophy of the aristocracy, to view it as being enclosed within the boundaries of that class would be to deny that system of thought its adaptive and expansive abilities.[61]

In this spread of Confucianism, distinctive schools of thought began to develop in Japan as lively philosophical debate emerged among scholars. The leaders of these schools of thought included those who were most indebted to the Song Neo-Confucian scholar Zhu Xi (such as Yamazaki Ansai and Hayashi Razan), others who were more attracted to the Ming Neo-Confucian Wang Yangming (such as Nakae Tōju and Kumazawa Banzan),[62] and still others who felt it was important to return to the early Confucian tradition of Confucius and Mencius (such as Itō Jinsai and Ogyū Sorai).[63] Numerous philosophical issues divided these schools, but a principal area of debate in Japan was the adaptability of Confucianism to a different cultural and intellectual milieu. The process of accommodating Confucianism to the Japanese context has been termed the naturalization of Confucianism.[64] It involved intricate and at times tortuous discussions of which aspects of Confucianism were appropriate to particular times, places, and circumstances in Japan. For certain thinkers it brought into focus ways in which Confucianism and Shinto could be compared, identified, or syncretized so as to indigenize Confucian ideas by means of the native tradition. As Najita has observed, for many of these scholars this process of adaptation was a means of giving a language and a vocabulary to an indigenous ethical system: Shinto.[65]

This process of adapting and adopting Confucian philosophy and practice was for Ekken a central concern. He attempted to address the issue on a number of levels, including showing the compatibility of Confucianism and Shinto and popularizing Confucian moral teachings among various classes in society. The issue of selectively adopting another philosophical tradition is a main concern in the *Record of Great Doubts*.

What is striking about Ekken's process of selectively adopting from the Chinese Neo-Confucian tradition is his long reflection on various aspects of Zhu Xi's thought and his reluctance to appear to break radically with him. Sometime after the age of thirty-five, Ekken became more fully convinced of the correctness of Zhu's ideas. Before that, he had read widely in the texts of Lu Xiangshan, Wang Yangming, and their followers. His turn from the Lu-Wang school to the Cheng-Zhu school occurred after his discovery of the *General Critique of Obscurations of Learning* (*Xue bu tong bian*) by Chen Jian (1497–1567). Chen's sharp critique of the Lu-Wang school as being too Buddhistic and subject to excesses helped to shape Ekken's allegiance to Zhu Xi. It also heightened his awareness of purported Buddhist influences on Zhu and the other Neo-Confucians. Nonetheless, to promote Zhu's thought Ekken compiled selections of his most critical passages and punctuated them so they could be read in Japanese. These were published in *A Selection of Zhu Xi's Writing* (*Shushi bunpan*) when Ekken was thirty-eight. Yet even from this time Ekken's doubts were evident, for it was this same year that he wrote *Notes on Reflections on Things at Hand*, in which he cited passages from Xue Xuan disagreeing with Zhu's understanding of principle and material force.[66] Ekken's doubts regarding Zhu's ideas became more pronounced in his late forties, and by the time he was fifty-six they appeared to be irresolvable.[67]

It is interesting to note, however, that he did not publish the *Record of Great Doubts* during his lifetime. The reasons for this may never be fully understood, but at a minimum it appears to reflect his concern that he would be identified with the Ancient Learning (*kogaku*) scholars, especially Itō Jinsai, who had adopted a position regarding *qi* close to his own. In their search for a pure form of Confucianism, the Ancient Learning scholars sought to return to the classical texts of Confucianism, especially Confucius and Mencius, and to bypass the later Neo-Confucian thinkers. Ekken seemed to feel that Jinsai was too critical of Zhu Xi, and he did not want to appear to be dismissive of Zhu's thought, as Jinsai was in his return to the early Confucian classics. Okada Takehiko has suggested, moreover, that Ekken felt a debt of gratitude to the Song Confucians because of their affirmation of the importance of a deep love of nature.[68] So much of Ekken's practical learning arose from his feeling for the complexity and beauty of nature. Accordingly, Ekken's gratitude to the Song Confucians, and to Zhu Xi in particular, is expressed with great deference. He strongly criticized the Ming Confucians, who seemed to Ekken to be arrogant and flippant in their disagreements with Zhu. Ekken chose as due respect for Zhu's teachings neither such disregard nor a blind loyalty but an appropriate and thoughtful disagreement with them.

Consequently, Ekken was reluctant to have the *Record of Great Doubts* published lest he be misunderstood as rejecting Zhu Xi. Even his followers were hesitant to publish the text after his death because they understood his concern that his thought could be dismissed as heretical. Not until half a century later was it finally published, by Ono Hokkai, one of Ogyū Sorai's disciples. The work was praised by Sorai when he first read it several years after Ekken's death: "It gives me great pleasure to find that there is a scholar in a faraway place who has anticipated my own thoughts."[69] Mori Rantaku, a disciple of Dazai Shundai, also praised the *Record of Great Doubts*: "The one volume of the *Taigiroku* is superlative, a comprehensive treatise which is the result of extensive scholarship and deep dedication. . . . This book alone sufficiently displays Ekken's greatness as a master. It is an ever-shining beacon of scholarship."[70]

It would seem, then, according to Okada Takehiko and others, that although the *Record of Great Doubts* was greatly appreciated by later scholars, Ekken's concern was he might be seen as too closely aligned with Jinsai's more radical critique and as having abandoned Zhu Xi. His disagreement with some of Zhu Xi's ideas left undiminished his profound debt to Zhu's synthesis of Song Neo-Confucianism, and Okada has thus called him a reformed Zhu Xi scholar.[71]

One of Ekken's underlying intentions was to identify the lingering traces of Buddhist and Daoist influences in Zhu's thought that seemed to him to tend toward emptiness and a lack of involvement in worldly affairs. In highlighting these influences, he hoped to maintain the important connection between cosmology and self-cultivation; his primary concern was that one's metaphysics should affect one's ethical stance in the world. Ideas and action, theory and practice were deeply intertwined. He made a valiant, though at times tortuous, effort to identify systematically what he felt was problematic in Zhu's metaphysics and ethics. This required, however, carefully defining the grounds for disagreement within a tradition. Setting the parameters of dissent between skepticism and blind acceptance was a major contribution of the *Record of Great Doubts*.

Tradition and the Individual: The Importance of Dissent and the Centrality of Learning

In religion, philosophy, and social thought, doubt and dissent have always had a crucial role, for ideas are rarely passed on without reflection and debate. In the West, from the early Greek skeptics to contemporary deconstructionists and postcolonialists, elements of dissent have continued to percolate and provoke. Similarly in Asia, from the Buddhist sense of great doubt in the Chan tradition to the skepticism and paradox of the Daoists and the intellectual questioning and investigations of the Confucians, doubt has been an ongoing preoccupation. This role of doubt serves to remind us of the constant elusiveness of truth and the volatility of traditions. It also underscores the creativity of individuals and the vitality of thought traditions that are open to discussion and dissent. The delicate balancing of individual doubt with the burden of the past is at the heart of the struggle of traditions over time and across cultures. Indeed, identifying the complex dynamics of change and continuity within a tradition is a major challenge for philosophers, theologians, and historians.

When a significant intellectual debate emerges in a tradition, it not only illuminates the tensions within and pressures from without, but also testifies to the vitality and flexibility of the tradition for the adherents themselves. Lines of doubt and argumentation cast light on the strands of continuity and change:

> When there is a prolonged and general loyalty to any complex philosophy, philosophical discourse tends to take on the character of fine-grained, exacting analysis and argumentation known as "scholasticism." This is a treasure for those interested in discovering the dynamic tensions and stresses that reveal the structural seams of a complex philosophical synthesis. As the fine grain emerges in a piece of wood through long polishing, so too does scholastic polishing inevitably bring out the fine grain of the system. And it is the controversies that resist solution that are most of interest; if there is some point that can engage fine minds on both sides for decades or even centuries, it likely indicates a deeper strain, conflict or tension in the very structure of the system itself.[72]

Examples of such creative tension are the different but complementary emphases of the Cheng-Zhu and Lu-Wang schools in China, the Four-Seven debate (on the Four Beginnings and the Seven Feelings) in Korea,[73] and the arguments regarding the relationship between principle and material force that characterize Neo-Confucian thought throughout East Asia. As we have seen, this debate regarding principle and material force was important in the work of Luo Qinshun in China, Yi Yulgok in Korea, and Kaibara Ekken in Japan.

For Ekken, this balancing of individual doubt and a tradition's lineage was a monumental preoccupation engaging many decades of his life. He did not want to subvert the transmission of the tradition or to undermine the contribution of his intellectual forebears. Rather, he hoped to enrich and enliven the multiple interpretations and implications of Confucian thought, especially that of Zhu Xi. Ekken's intellectual struggles cause us to reevaluate the conventional notion that Confucianism was a tradition transmitted routinely without disagreement or individual reflection. Moreover, it adds complexity to the various divisions of orthodox and heterodox teachings in Confucianism by suggesting that the dividing lines were not clearly drawn and that criteria for categorization were subject to continual contestation and reevaluation. In short, the subtlety of the means and methods of dissent in a figure like Ekken demand a more careful reflection on issues of intellectual lineage and transmission as well as creativity and change within a tradition like Confucianism. Such reflection requires us to focus again on the role of learning for Confucians.

Because learning is central to the Confucian tradition, the content and method of learning were frequently the source of discussion and debate. As the Confucians created a sense of correct historical lineage of the passage of the Dao, as they established schools or encouraged study in the family, as they fostered civil service examinations or promoted government service, some of the key questions and concerns surrounded the topic of learning.[74]

Within these discussions there arose a creative tension between learning as a communal legacy and learning as individually liberating. In other words, the dialectic between the tradition and the individual was a source of constant interplay and reflection. The changes and continuities in the tradition can be traced to the manifold debates on the centrality of learning. Education was a means of sifting through past inheritance and present concerns for personal rectification as well as for societal needs. Scholars were inspired by the ideal of learning in order to improve themselves rather than to impress others. To suggest, as some scholars have, that Confucianism promoted only rote memorization or rigid traditionalism is to overlook many of the subtleties and differences in the process of learning that occurred in different historical times, geographical spaces, and cultural circumstances.

The Confucian emphasis on learning for the improvement of the individual as well as society resulted in a remarkable flourishing of what Wm. Theodore de Bary has called Confucian personalism, by which the self was seen not as an isolated individual but as "the dynamic center of a larger social whole, biological continuum, and moral/spiritual continuity."[75] Critical to this Confucian personalism was a commitment to learning and to scholarly pursuits, a commitment that distinguished Confucianism as a tradition and galvanized individuals toward a path of "learning for oneself."[76] This ideal of learning for oneself implied a deeply felt sense of personal realization along with the potential for finding the Way (Dao) in oneself.[77] The passion for learning as a means of transforming self and society no doubt accounts for the remarkable appeal and affirmation of Confucianism across the cultures and societies of East Asia.

In essence, learning was the vehicle toward cultivation of the individual that would in turn affect the family, the society, the state, and even the cosmos. This is most succinctly expressed in the *Great Learning*, which Zhu Xi selected from the *Record of Rites* as one of the Four Books essential to any educational curriculum. Hence learning was an activity with great moral and spiritual import. It was not undertaken only for one's own edification, but for the positive effects on the larger social-political milieu. Through learning, appropriate harmonious relations could be activated between self and society and between individuals and the natural world. In addition, practical learning would benefit the larger society.

Tradition: Legacy, Lineage, and Learning

For Ekken the dialectic between tradition and the individual was a delicate but dynamic one. Learning for him was a lifelong personal commitment to the Confucian Way as well as a means for the appropriation of Confucian ideas for the political, social, and educational realms. How to adapt and adopt the Confucian tradition preoccupied Ekken throughout his life. This is especially evident in his moral treatises, which were intended to spread Confucian teachings to various groups and classes in Tokugawa society.

The *Record of Great Doubts* bears the fruit of this preoccupation in a carefully constructed document. Although the lines of argumentation are frequently repetitive, Ekken asserts his loyalty to the tradition while demonstrating his ability to dissent from it. This kind of creative dissent is the means by which the Confucian tradition was changed and adapted to new circumstances. It does not approach outright skepticism, but it exhibits its own method of careful inquiry.

This method is evident in Ekken's urging that distinctions should be made among (1) particular texts, (2) key individuals, (3) significant ideas, and (4) types of scholarship. He notes first that the classical texts are the most reliable, especially the *Classic of Changes*. Moreover, the language of the classics is, he asserts, significant and should be followed carefully. He takes an example from the *Classic of Changes* of the Chinese character for "one" in describing yin and yang as a basis for discussing his unified philosophy of the Way. Second, he argues that one should have respect for individuals in the tradition but should also realize that people have blind spots and are not infallible. Thus, for example, the Song scholars may be sagacious but they are not sages. In this respect, the learning of Confucius and Mencius is considered sagely, while that of the Song Neo-Confucians is deemed wise. Third, he believes the ideas of the Song Confucians that rely on Confucius and Mencius should be distinguished from those not rooted in Confucius and Mencius. In this way, one can identify some of the underlying Buddhist and Daoist influences on Song Neo-Confucianism, especially with regard to meditation and quietism. Fourth, Ekken judges that Song scholarship is too detailed, verbose, and scattered when compared with the holistic theories of Confucius and Mencius. He suggests that a scholar ought to start with things close at hand and proceed to more lofty things.

Individual Learning: Doubting, Discerning, Deciding

Ekken's notion of doubt as a method of inquiry into the tradition and discernment as a means of selectivity within the tradition is complemented by the idea of deciding for oneself as a means of re-appropriation of the tradition. All of this depends primarily on the persistence and perception of an individual in pursuing learning. Doubting, discerning, and deciding are the key tools in acquiring knowledge of the Way. Without these tools the tradition could become a stagnant repository of platitudes rather than an enlivened stream of intellectual resources.

Ekken also observes that the *Classic of Changes* reminds us that the Way is vast and no individual alone can exhaust it. One needs to consult with others who are broad-minded and to place confidence in one's teachers. Complete self-reliance or subjectivity, he points out, would be inappropriate to the challenging task of pursuing the Way.

The individual is encouraged above all to acknowledge that doubt—appropriate rather than simply trivial doubt—is an indispensable intellectual tool. Ekken's text opens with a positive view of doubt as promoting progress in learning. A statement included from Zhu Xi underscores this: "If our doubt is great, our progress will be significant; if our doubt is small, our progress will be insignificant. If we don't have doubts, we won't progress."[78] Indeed, we are told, as Lu Xiangshan said, "In learning it is regrettable if we do not have doubts."[79] Throughout the text, we are urged to move through the process of doubt and discernment to decision making so that "we should doubt what we should doubt and believe what we should believe."

Ekken describes this process as one of various stages that may occur in sequence or in a multifold simultaneity. Discernment involves choosing and discarding particular ideas by sifting carefully through various alternatives. This demands having an openness to learning and abandoning self-concern. It requires avoiding narrowness, obstinacy, or bias in one's view. It also implies that one should not be too critical, arrogant, or aggressive in stating one's opinions.[80] Ekken specifically criticizes the Ming Confucians in this regard. He suggests, rather, that one needs to express one's ideas with sympathy and sincerity.

Finally, one ought, Ekken notes, to develop the habits of good scholarship: accessibility and simplicity, not abstraction and abstruseness. When all these tools are being applied one can decide for oneself what is appropriate learning within a tradition. One can then follow the Way and adapt its pursuit to one's own time, place, and circumstances. Accordingly, inquiring, selecting, and reappropriating are the means for the individual to interact creatively with tradition.

It is instructive to see how Ekken's own text exemplifies his probing method of discernment in terms of both content and style. In particular, the repetition of certain ideas and key phrases clearly have a function of highlighting his main concerns. His style also demonstrates a spirit of open scholarly inquiry along with an invitational tone to the reader to reflect together with Ekken on these issues. Moreover, through repetition an honesty and humility of painstaking rumination are conveyed. Doubting is never complete for Ekken, and, rather like recurring musical cadences, the repetition of doubt reflects stylized permutations with an underlying purpose. Indeed, as a method of inquiry, repetition in the Confucian tradition can be seen as the "practice of learning,"[81] one requiring attention and provoking reformulation.

Philosophical Debates Regarding Principle and Material Force

The Nature of the Disagreements with Zhu Xi

Ekken's disagreements with Zhu Xi focused on the issue of cosmology, in particular the nature and formation of the universe. While this may appear to be simply a rarefied metaphysical discussion, its implications for his ethical thought and his studies of nature are far from abstract. From Ekken's naturalism outlined as a philosophy of material force, he is able to argue for an affirmation of human nature and human action along with an appreciation of the natural world and its seasonal transformations.

Ekken wished to affirm the unity of the dynamic creativity of the processes of nature and of the Way. He maintained that the processes of nature and of the Way flowed from the same generative source of material force and argued that they could not emerge from what he understood to be the original emptiness referred to by Buddhists and Daoists. He quoted the *Doctrine of the Mean* to illustrate his point: "The great Way of the sages is vast and it causes the development and growth of all things."[82] Ekken continues, "It flows through the seasons and never stops. It is the root of all transformations and the place from which all things emerge. It is the origin of all that is received from Heaven."[83]

Ekken claimed that the Cheng brothers and Zhu Xi had set forth a qualified but dualistic position that tended to separate the Way from concrete reality. He maintained that Zhu argued for the differentiation of *li* and *qi*. This resulted in a potential bifurcation of this world and a transcendent realm. Ekken firmly denied that this was consonant with a Confucian sense of the importance of commitment to the world. He argued against such a dualism because he felt it could lead to an idealism that undervalued nature and human action in the world and thus could result in life-denying rather than life-affirming ethical practices.

Ekken argued for a naturalism that saw the universe as emerging and continuing due solely to the operations of material force. He emphasized the unity of this dynamic life process, for it is understanding and harmonizing with this vital force that forms the basis of moral and spiritual cultivation.

The Implications of a Vitalistic Cosmology of Material Force

It is important to note that what distinguishes Song Neo-Confucianism from earlier Confucianism is a more elaborate attention to cosmology and metaphysics. Zhu Xi's Neo-Confucian synthesis in *Reflections on Things at Hand* begins with a section titled "On the Substance of the Way," which draws on Zhou Dunyi's cosmological "Explanation of the Diagram of the Supreme Ultimate." This diagram and Zhu's interpretation of it became the source of Ekken's doubts regarding Zhu's metaphysics.

In the *Record of Great Doubts*, Ekken gives careful attention to Zhu Xi's interpretation of the "Explanation of the Diagram of the Supreme Ultimate" as a cosmological map of evolution. Ekken's aim was to distinguish elements in the diagram he felt were Buddhist or Daoist. His concern related especially to two points that, in Ekken's mind, illustrate the implications of the interconnection of cosmology and cultivation in a way that could devalue action in the world:

1. The cosmogonic problem of the origins of the universe as seen in the relation of *wuji* (nonfinite) and *taiji* (Supreme Ultimate) as either bifurcating reality or as suggesting that the

source of all reality is emptiness. *Wuji* has been translated as the Ultimate of Nonbeing, the nonfinite, or the infinite, while *taiji* has been translated as the Great Ultimate or the Supreme Ultimate. Joseph Adler has translated them as Non-Polar (*wuji*) and Supreme Polarity (*taiji*).[84]

2. The relationship of these two polarities reflects the ethical problem of potentially prioritizing tranquility and thus emphasizing withdrawal from affairs.

These two points were, in fact, criticized by others before Ekken, often for similar reasons. Perhaps the most famous disagreement occurred in a series of debates between Zhu Xi and Lu Xiangshan over the *wuji–taiji* issue. Ekken concisely summarizes the problem: "The Supreme Ultimate [*taiji*] originates from the nonfinite [*wuji*] and thus establishes making quietude central as the fundamental mode for humans. These concepts have been transmitted from Buddhism and Daoism."[85]

Okada Takehiko has outlined the points of Ekken's disagreements with Zhu Xi:

[T]he doctrine of the Supreme Ultimate and the Infinite (*t'ai-chi wu-chi*; *taikyoku mukyoku*), the doctrine of abiding in tranquility, the doctrine of quiet-sitting, the identification of nature with principle, the distinction between an original nature and a physical nature, the dualism of principle and material force, the idea of the indestructibility of principle and the nature, the idea of clear virtue as tranquil and unobscured, the idea of the Principle of Nature as empty, tranquil and without any sign, the idea of one source for substance and function, and the idea of the identity of the manifest and the hidden.[86]

The opening line of the "Explanation of the Diagram of the Supreme Ultimate" is "The Ultimate of Non-Being (*wuji*) and also the

Great Ultimate (*taiji*)."[87] This line refers to the origin of all life and has been subject to numerous interpretations and debates. The central problem in the debate is the role of *wuji* and its relation to *taiji*. The problem is exacerbated by the ambiguity of the linking word *er*, which means "and also" or "in turn." It can likewise be translated as "and then," which implies a separation between these two entities. Zhu Xi's comments on this line imply that he is trying to hold these two terms in creative tension:

> "The operations of Heaven have neither sound nor smell." And yet this [Ultimate of Nonbeing] is really the axis of creation and the foundation of things of all kinds [ultimate being]. Therefore "the Ultimate of Nonbeing and also the Great Ultimate." It does not mean that outside of the Great Ultimate there is an Ultimate of Nonbeing.[88]

It should be noted that Wm. Theodore de Bary has argued that Zhu Xi did not use *wuji* as simply a Daoist principle of emptiness out of which reality emerged. Rather, he suggests that "*wuji* and *taiji* were inseparable aspects, not successive stages of being. They were correlative aspects of a Way that was in one sense indeterminate and yet in another sense the supreme value and ultimate end of all things."[89] The implications of this are significant for the link between cosmological principles and self-cultivation. The Supreme Ultimate, or principle, is manifest in each individual human nature. However, the cultivation of this opens one up to the inexhaustible potential of boundless creativity. Thus for Zhu Xi, the human mind is "empty and spiritual yet replete with principle."[90]

The dynamic relationships between the cosmological principles of *wuji* and *taiji* and their implications for self-cultivation are at the heart of Ekken's concerns. Even if, as de Bary argues, Zhu Xi did not intend *wuji* to be equated with emptiness, Ekken was nonetheless particularly worried that *wuji* may be perceived as comparable to emptiness or nothingness in a Buddhist or Daoist sense. The difficulty Ekken saw issuing from this perspective is that by positing *wuji* as the foundation of everything, one may tend to see the myriad things that arise as illusory and quietism may be a consequence. This is Ekken's principal concern as he questions the origins of the Diagram of the Supreme Ultimate and the uses of the term *wuji*. Ekken notes that while Zhou employs the term in the "Explanation of the Diagram of the Supreme Ultimate," he does not refer to it in *Penetrating the Classic of Changes*. He suggests that the Cheng brothers never used the term *wuji*. In noting its Daoist and Buddhist links, however, he claims the term appears first in Daoism in *Laozi* (chap. 28) and then in Buddhism in the *Huayan View of the Realm of the Dharmas* (*Huayan fajie guan*) of Dushun (557–640).[91]

Ekken emphasized instead the importance of *taiji*, identifying it with a primal *qi*, as had Zhang Zai. This differed from Zhu Xi's identification of it with *li*, which he considered ontologically prior to material force. Zhu also claimed that *wuji* is necessary because without it "*taiji* will be on the same level as things and thus we can't regard it as the origin of the transformation in all things."[92] Ekken disagreed, saying one needed to preserve a unified vital material force as the basis of existence. For him, *taiji* is material force in a state of chaos before yin and yang separated. In relation to the creation of things in the universe in concrete form, Ekken makes an important ontological distinction between what is above form (in Heaven) and what is below (on Earth). "Above form" is yin and yang and their alterations, which result in concrete things "below." Yin and yang are not within physical forms but are above forms, as suggested in the *Classic of Changes*. This means that phenomena arise through the movement of yin and yang in Heaven, not within physical form.

According to Ekken, what is above form is the material force of yin and yang. These polarities are manifest in their operation of ceaseless alteration. This is called the Dao, or the boundless source of all reality—indeed, the wellspring of creativity in the universe. Ekken observes that yin and yang flow and alternate, and this causes growth in all things.[93]

Ekken's criticism of Zhu Xi and the Cheng brothers is that, by placing yin and yang within concrete things, they divided yin and yang from the Way. They also necessarily separated principle and material force and identified principle with the Way and material force with yin and yang. The danger of suggesting that yin and yang are within the realm of concrete things is it can lead to abstraction of the Way as separate from concrete reality and the bifurcation of principle from material force.

Summarizing his objections, Ekken states: "To regard nothingness as the origin and fundamental spirit of all things is a Buddhist and Daoist idea. To regard existence as the origin and essence of all things is the teachings of the sages. Here the explanations concerning existence and nonexistence are the dividing line between the Way of the sages and other paths."[94]

Ekken was concerned that such a dualism could result in an idealism that undervalued concrete objects in the world and tended toward life-denying rather than life-affirming practices. In supporting his own arguments against dualism, he frequently cited Luo Qinshu's formulation, "Principle is one, its particularizations are diverse." He also relied on Luo's phrase "principle is the principle of material force"[95] to suggest that principle is not separate from or prior to material force. Nor, Ekken asserted, is it eternal and unchanging. On this point, he disagreed with Zhu Xi, who said that while material force was subject to the transformation of life and death, principle was not.[96] Ekken saw principle as existing within material force, but principle is destroyed when something dies.

Ekken argued for a vitalistic naturalism according to which the fecundity of the universe arises from a primal flow of material force. Above forms this primal energy is the interaction of yin and yang, while within the realm of forms it courses through all reality. Ekken relied on the *Classic of Changes* to distill his position on the unifying vitality of material force as the source of generation and transformation.

Ekken's cosmological and metaphysical concerns carried over to his views on human nature and ethical practice. Like Luo, he did not feel one should make distinctions between an original nature (usually seen as perfect) and a physical nature (usually seen as imperfect). Following Luo, Ekken argued that the nature conferred by Heaven was not separate from physical nature. If there was a division, how could one account for the origin of physical nature? He believed that the Heavenly endowed human nature one receives is principle. According to Mencius, human nature is essentially good and all people receive the innate "seeds" of commiseration, shame, modesty, and conscience, which, when cultivated, lead to virtues.[97] Differences arise in humans due to the varied nature of the material force they receive.

Ekken again called on Luo's formula, "Principle is one, its particularizations are diverse," to suggest that, in relation to human nature, original form and distinctive characteristics are not two separate things. The implications of Ekken's unified view of human nature were twofold: (1) to affirm rather than deny the emotions and (2) to emphasize loyalty and sincerity rather than austere reverence or intense seriousness. With regard to emotions, Ekken urged the appropriate and timely expression of feelings. Similarly, he discouraged the forced effort of restraint brought on by overseriousness in ethical practice or scholarly endeavors. Ekken promoted instead the need to cultivate sincerity in human life, for it reflected the sincerity of the Way of Heaven in its natural rhythms and seasonal cycles. For him sincerity was fundamental, while seriousness was a secondary artifact of practice that too often led to rigidity and distance from others.

The purpose of self-cultivation was to remove this kind of separation of oneself from others so that one's heart could embrace all things. In this way, humaneness is activated and one is able to "form one body with all things." These ideas were as important for Ekken as for the Song and Ming Neo-Confucians before him. He was particularly moved by the celebration of experiencing Heaven, Earth, and all things as one body in Zhang Zai's *Western Inscription*.

Ekken viewed this identification of humans with "the ten thousand things" as reflecting the dynamic process of the flow of material force in both the individual and nature. As one cultivates humaneness, Ekken explained, one participates in this nourishing energy of material force: "Grass and trees are produced ceaselessly and, similarly, within our hearts the originative process of nature flourishes and is an endless source of joyful energy—this is happiness."[98] He emphasized the value of feeling and enjoying the beauty of nature, which would nourish one's natural contentment. By engaging and nourishing oneself in this way, one could resonate with the processes of growth and transformation in nature. The generative power of nature reflects the workings of Heaven (*tenki*).[99] This call to participate in the transformations in the universe harkens back to the *Doctrine of the Mean*, which states that such participation reflects the sincerity of the Way of Heaven. Ekken observes: "Every year without fail, from ancient times to the present, the sun and moon have circulated, the four seasons have changed, and numerous things have been born. This is the sincerity of the Heavenly Way, and should be revered. Those who are peaceful and experience this will have a deep joy; those who fully understand this truth will know the Way."[100]

As is evident in this passage, Ekken was deeply moved by a sense of vitality in nature reflected in the joy of humans. What distinguishes his thought in this regard is his sense of profound indebtedness to nature for its dynamic gift of life. He is continually celebrating the fecundity of the universe and simultaneously suggesting that humans should acknowledge their debt to nature as the source and sustainer of life and repay it through service to society:

> Nature gives birth to all and supplies each person with the means to perform his function. From the highest government officer to the lowliest workman, each is accorded the ability to benefit society in his own measure. Great Heaven gives birth to us all and we are deeply indebted to it. It has given us all the necessary means for obtaining the requisite food, clothing, shelter, and means for making a living. The debt we owe to Heaven is apparent in all aspects of our existence and is so great that we can never fully repay it. All we can do to repay even the most minute fraction of the debt is to act in accord with the will of Heaven and attempt to benefit man.[101]

Ekken urges people to extend the virtue of filiality beyond the sphere of the family to embrace Heaven and Earth, the Great Parents of all things. Nature should be respected and cared for, not exploited. Underlying Ekken's thinking is his view of the unity of life in its myriad forms due to the dynamic presence of material force. Any tendency to bifurcate *qi* and *li* risked, he believed, devaluing this world, abstracting human action, and fossilizing moral cultivation. By affirming the dynamic sincerity of the Way as reflected in the human practice of sincerity, Ekken showed a means for avoiding such risks. The gravity for Ekken of such risks accounts for the importance he placed on the monism of *qi* as a basis for a coherent metaphysics and ethics.

Reappropriating Tradition: Practical Learning and the Philosophy of *Qi*

As a leading Neo-Confucian scholar in early modern Japan, Ekken's contributions to Tokugawa discourse were manifold, embracing a

broad spectrum of concerns ranging from the intellectual intrica-
cies of Neo-Confucian philosophy to the popularization of moral
teachings and to practical learning involving agriculture and botany.
In all these efforts, Ekken was indebted to particular aspects of the
Confucian and Neo-Confucian traditions. Yet he was able to selectively adapt the tradition to the needs of his time, place, and circumstances. Indeed, he is a prime example of the adaptability and appeal of Neo-Confucian ideas and practice across East Asian cultures.
His ability to both affirm and dissent from the leading synthesizer
of Neo-Confucianism, Zhu Xi, reveals the dynamic characteristics
of the tradition.

The *Record of Great Doubts* remains a key document exemplifying
this dialectic of internal debate and reappropriation of tradition with
philosophical, historical, religious, and practical implications. As a
text advocating a philosophy of material force, it reflects the significant philosophical discussions on cosmology and ethics that preoccupied many Neo-Confucian scholars in China, Korea, and Japan. It
helps us to trace the historical movements of these dialogues across
East Asia.[102] It underscores the religious concerns of the tradition
in terms of issues of self-cultivation and participation in the social,
political, and cosmological orders. Finally, it undergirds the preoccupation with practical learning, which some commentators have
described as "empirical rationalism."[103] The implications of this rationalism for understanding Japan's modernization process have
been suggested by Minamoto Ryōen.[104] A full analysis of this subject awaits further exploration as more texts are translated and the
richness of the various currents of premodern Japanese intellectual
history becomes more widely understood.

Many questions attend such a study, for the implications of
Ekken's ideas and methodology are significant in a number of areas. For example, there are questions to be explored regarding the
influence of Neo-Confucian thought on education in the Tokugawa
period and on the rapid modernization process in Japan in the past

150 years. Many scholars acknowledge that the high rate of literacy in Japan by the mid-nineteenth century is attributable in large measure to the effectiveness of Confucian education during the previous 250 years.[105] A conclusion from this is that there was an educated public ready for the task of modernization and already skilled at adapting ideas from abroad, primarily from China and Korea.

In this context of what constitutes modernity or the conditions of modernization, other questions arise regarding the emergence of science and rationalism in Japan along with traditional Neo-Confucian cosmology and ethics. In this vein, some interpreters regard Ekken as an incipient rationalist and materialist because of his monism of *qi* and his interest in practical learning. They see his thought leading toward a kind of logical positivism that objectifies nature so as to study it. In this context, they view Ekken as part of a movement toward a secular modernity that leaves religious concerns behind. This underscores, however, the need to examine whether the emergence of the scientific method requires the objectification of the natural world and whether science implies a lack of interest in ethics or religion. Does science demand a separation, as Maruyama Masao has implied, of norm and nature or of ethics and empiricism?[106] Does science or Enlightenment thinking require a dualism of self and the world such that "spirit" needs to be removed from nature? These issues, while critical and currently being debated in many circles, are beyond the scope of this study. Nonetheless, I wish to briefly explore some of the interpretations of Ekken's ideas in this context.[107]

It is important to note here that a key contribution of Ekken's thought is precisely that for him *qi* was a basis of both ethical cultivation and empirical exploration of the natural world. They were not seen as two separate things but as part of the long practice of cultivation encouraged in the Neo-Confucian tradition for centuries. In particular, a person was urged to "abide in reverence" within and to "investigate things" without (*jujing, gewu*). In this practice, there was the common understanding that such investigation meant "exploring principle" (*qiongli*), seeing the pattern, shape, and order of things. Thus, for example, Ekken's taxonomic study of nature in its great variety—flowers, plants, fish, birds, shells—was within the larger Neo-Confucian tradition of examining nature and classifying life-forms.

Whether this investigation is termed natural history or taxonomic science, its impulse was toward an empirical understanding of the principle of things. For Ekken, and for other Tokugawa Neo-Confucians who took up studies of human anatomy through Western books imported from Nagasaki, the motivation was learning not only for oneself but for the larger society as well. This was known as *jitsugaku*, or practical learning. The breadth of Ekken's practical learning was remarkably wide, as the Japanese Confucian scholar Okada Takehiko has observed: "The scope of Ekken's *jitsugaku* was truly amazing, covering everything from the experience and practice of ethics to manners, institutions, linguistics, medicine, botany, zoology, agriculture, production, taxonomy, food, sanitation, law, mathematics (computation), music, and military tactics."[108] Astronomy, geography, history, and genealogy can be added to this list.

In all his studies, Ekken advocated a practical learning that would foster personal cultivation while also assisting others: both self and society benefited. In this spirit, he urged that learning should be "preserved in the heart and carried out in action" (*juyō no gaku*).[109] Like many Confucian scholars, he studied astronomy not only to understand the movement of the stars but also to assist in calendar reforms. In contrast to many Confucians who saw the study of mathematics as suitable for only the merchant class, he promoted learning mathematics for management of the household, of agriculture, and of the government. He encouraged the study of plants and horticulture to improve agricultural techniques as well as to understand nature's generative processes. This combination of principle and practicality, of appreciation and application distinguishes

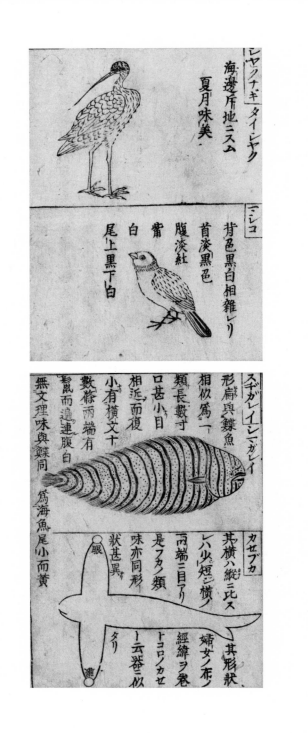

海邊斤地ニスム
夏月味美

レヤクナキ｜タイ｜レヤク

背色黒白相雑レリ
首淡黒色
腹淡紅
膚
白
尾上黒下白

ニシコ

形扁與鰈魚
相似爲一
類長數寸
口甚小目
相近而復
小有横文十
數條兩端有
鼠而遶連腹白
無文理味與鰈同
爲海魚尾小而黄

スヂガレイ｜ニシガレイ

其横八縦ニ比ス
其形狀
レハ少短シ横ノ
婦女ノ布ノ
兩端ニ目アリ
經緯ヲ巻
是フカノ類
トコロノカセ
味亦同形
一云碁ニ似
狀甚異
タリ

カセブカ

眼

蓮

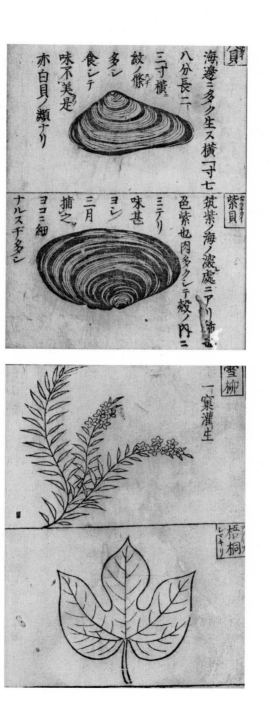

海邊ニ多ク生ス横「寸七
八分長二寸
二寸横二
故ノ條
多シ
食シテ
味不美是
亦白貝ノ類ナリ

紫貝

筑紫ノ海ノ淺處ニアリ希
色紫也肉多クシテ殻ノ内ニ
ミテリ
味甚
ヨシ
三月
捕之ノ
ヨコニ細
ナルスヂ多シ

苙柳

一窠灌生

梧桐

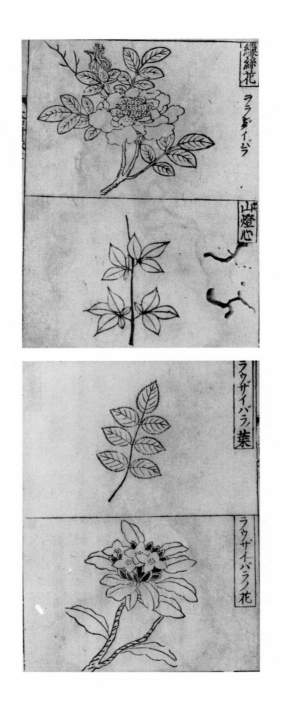

Ekken's thought. This dynamic synthesis was based on his philosophy of *qi*, which aimed to nourish life (*yōjō no jutsu*)—both within and without.[110]

Ekken's *Plants of Japan* (*Yamato honzō*), published in 1709, has been called the first systematic botanical text produced in Japan. It captured the admiration of Westerners who came to Japan after it was opened to the West at the end of the nineteenth century. While based on the taxonomical compilation of the Chinese Ming scholar Li Shizhen (1518–1593), it went beyond Li's investigation of trees, plants, and flowers to include birds, fish, and shells. Ekken described in detail over 1,550 objects, bringing together his constant concern to celebrate nature's fecundity, as he indicates in the preface, with a desire to benefit society as a whole. Okada has summarized the importance of Ekken's contribution: "He absorbed, modified, and surpassed the traditional Chinese herbological studies, applying the principle with creative insight to the Japanese context in his *Yamato honzō*, which had an enormous influence on the development of later pharmacological, botanical, and zoological research in Japan."[111]

Interpretations of Ekken's Philosophy of *Qi*

In his practical learning, Ekken's unified embrace of material force, of matter and spirit, is constantly evident. It has, however, been commonplace to describe modernity and modern consciousness as arising in the West from a division of matter and spirit, of science and religion, of reason and faith. The apparent separation of rationalism and belief has been seen to be one of the factors leading to the rise of science and secularism in contrast to religion and spirituality. This somewhat simplistically described dualism is based on the assumption that the division of norm from nature makes possible modern thought free from traditional restraints. In other words, the study of ethics is regarded as separate from the empirical study of nature.

This conventional understanding has led several twentieth-century Japanese thinkers to see Ekken, through the lens of the *Record of Great Doubts*, as a decidedly modern thinker. This interpretation was especially championed by Maruyama Masao in *Studies in the Intellectual History of Tokugawa Japan*, first published in Japan in the 1940s.[112] Maruyama saw Ekken, along with Ogyū Sorai, as a philosopher who was able to break from the intertwined morality and metaphysics of Zhu Xi's Neo-Confucianism. He thus claimed Ekken as a modern rationalist and secular thinker apart from the medieval East Asian worldview dominated by traditional Confucian thought. Maruyama was critical of the premodern "continuative consciousness" of Confucianism, which he felt inhibited the emergence of modern critical consciousness. For him, such a modern consciousness was distinguished by the values of democratic individualism and the power to dissent. He sought these characteristics in the intellectual history of Japan amid the rise of fascism. Maruyama's influence has been significant, and several other prominent Japanese scholars have followed this interpretation, including Abe Yoshio and Minamoto Ryōen. This interpretive framework has resulted in the obfuscation of Ekken's distinctive contribution: the unifying perspective provided by his philosophy of material force.

In his study of the influence of Korean Confucianism in Japan, Abe divided Japanese Neo-Confucianism into two categories: the school of principle (*rigaku*) and the school of material force (*kigaku*).[113] *Rigaku*, he has suggested, was concerned with spirituality and ethics, since it embraced *ri* as a transcendent principle. *Kigaku*, in his view, was more inclined toward materialism and was concerned with broad practical learning. This division is not descriptive of Ekken, however, who had a unified view of spirit and matter in his *kigaku* philosophy.[114] It is precisely his embrace of both ethics and empiricism, reverence within and investigation without, that makes him distinctive and yet rooted in the deep impulses of the Neo-Confucian tradition.

Minamoto also follows this separation of ethical cultivation and rational investigation. He identifies two kinds of practical learning: the moral idealism of Nakae Tōju and Yamazaki Ansai and the empirical realism of Kaibara Ekken and Ogyū Sorai. Yet these categories do not adequately describe Ekken's more inclusive thought. Both Minamoto and Maruyama recognized the limits of these dualistic categories, but they suggest that the problem is in the contradictions of Ekken's thought rather than in the limits of the categories themselves.

This bifurcating analysis has also influenced Tetsuo Najita's interpretation of Ekken. He has described the significance of the *Record of Great Doubts* as "a pioneering statement of a trend within Tokugawa Neo-Confucianism that seeks a more empirical approach to the study of nature unfettered by the constrictions of metaphysical ethics."[115] Najita sees the life principle (*seiri*) in Ekken's thought as simply natural, not ethical. He claims that Ekken "stripped nature of explicit ethical content"[116] and came to "an essentially materialistic conclusion about the nature of the universe."[117] This is inconsistent, however, with Ekken's continual celebration of the creativity of the universe (origination) as comparable to the creativity in humans (humaneness).

In trying to reconcile the fact that norm and nature were not split in Ekken's thought, Najita concedes that they coexisted. He writes that "a commitment to Confucian ethics and to an empirical approach to nature concurred, each valid and each as important as the other."[118] Najita attempts to explain this coexistence in terms of substance and function (*ti–yong*). He sees ethics as substance and science as function, mutually separate and distinctive. It would be more accurate to conclude that, in Ekken's characterization, they are mutually reinforcing and supportive. Najita acknowledges that Ekken "argued that reverence for nature was a universal human capacity and constituted the ultimate basis for self-reflection regarding the moral character of human beings."[119] Clearly, for Ekken the vital force of the universe could be cultivated in the self, activated in society, and appreciated in nature.

To gain an understanding of how Ekken viewed these intersecting circles of self, society, and nature, it is important to situate his cosmological discussions in the broad context of Confucian naturalism. In so doing, I wish to point toward the larger implications of Ekken's ideas for some of our own contemporary concerns while recognizing the historical particularity of his text and context.

Confucian Cosmology:
Organic Holism and Dynamic Vitalism

In East Asia, naturalism as a primary ingredient of Neo-Confucianism is characterized by an organic holism and by a dynamic vitalism. This cosmological sensibility forms an important basis of Confucianism and gives rise to a distinctive understanding of ethics and self-cultivation. Ekken is clearly part of this tradition of holism and vitalism and yet goes ever further to emphasize the importance of material force as a basis for creative self-cultivation in harmony with nature.

In describing Confucianism as characterized by organic holism, reference is to the fact that the universe is viewed as an integrated unit and not as discrete mechanistic parts. The universe is seen as unified, interconnected, and interpenetrating. Everything interacts with and affects everything else, which is why the notion of microcosm and macrocosm is so essential to Confucian cosmology. The elaboration of the interconnectedness of reality can be seen in the correspondence of the elements with seasons, direction, colors, and even virtues. This system of correlative correspondences began sometime in the third millennium B.C.E. and resulted in texts such as the *Classic of Changes*. It was further elaborated by Han Confucians, such as Dong Zhongshu, and it remained an important aspect of Neo-Confucian thinking for nearly a millennium down to the modern period. In this context of correspondences, the relation of the person as microcosm to the universe as macrocosm is a central theme arising directly from this underlying idea of organic wholeness.

This interconnected quality has been described by Tu Weiming as a "continuity of being."[120] This implies a kind of great chain of being linking inorganic, organic, and human life-forms. For the Confucians, this linkage is a reality because of the fact that all life is constituted of *qi*, the material force or psychophysical element of the universe. It is the unifying element of the cosmos and constitutes the basis for a profound reciprocity between humans and the natural world.

In addition to organic holism, Confucian cosmology is characterized by a dynamic vitalism inherent in *qi*. Although this concept is present in early Confucian thought, as evidenced in thinkers such as Mencius, Neo-Confucians such as Luo Qinshun, Yi Yulgok, and Kaibara Ekken in particular underscore the importance of *qi* and its relation to *li*. The seventeenth-century scholar Wang Fuzhi described material force in the following manner:

> The fact that the things of the world, whether rivers or mountains, plants or animals, those with or without intelligence, and those yielding blossoms or bearing fruits, provide beneficial support for all things is the result of the natural influence of the moving power of material force. It fills the universe. And as it completely provides for the flourish and transformation of all things, it is all the more spatially unrestricted. As it is not spatially restricted, it operates in time and proceeds with time. From morning to evening, from spring to summer, and from the present tracing back to the past, there is no time at which it does not operate, and there is no time at which it does not produce.[121]

In Neo-Confucian thought, and in the philosophy of *qi* in particular, it is material force as the substance of life that is the basis for the continuing process of change and transformation in the universe. The term *sheng sheng* (life, life) is repeatedly used in Neo-Confucian texts to illustrate the ongoing creativity and renewal of nature. This recognition of the ceaseless movement of the cosmos arises from a profound meditation on the fecundity of nature in continually giving birth to new life. Furthermore, the use of the term *sheng sheng*, which means "production and reproduction," indicates an awareness that change is the basis for the interaction and continuation of the web of life systems—mineral, vegetable, animal, and human. And finally, the term celebrates transformation as the clearest expression of the creative processes of life, processes with which humans should harmonize their own actions. In essence, human beings are urged to "model themselves on the ceaseless vitality of the cosmic process."[122] This approach is an important key to Neo-Confucian thought, for a sense of holism, vitalism, and harmonizing with change provides the metaphysical basis on which an integrated morality can be developed. This was essential to Ekken's thought and why he argued for a monism of *qi*.

Confucian Cultivation: Harmonizing with Change and Assisting Transformation

For the Neo-Confucians, the idea of self-cultivation implied, as Tu Weiming has written, a "creative transformation."[123] Such a transformation of the human can be elaborated only in the context of an understanding of Neo-Confucian views of nature as already outlined. The view of the universe as organic, whole, dynamic, and vital has a direct bearing on the understanding of the moral and spiritual formation of human beings and on their action in the world.

In coming to understand Neo-Confucian self-cultivation as creative transformation, it should be noted that the essential metaphor for humans in relation to the cosmos is expressed in the idea of humans forming one body with Heaven and Earth: namely, the universe. This anthropocosmic worldview of a dynamic triad underlies the assumption of the human interconnectedness to all reality and acts also as an overriding goal of self-cultivation. The triad is both a given state at birth and an achievement to be realized over a lifetime of cultivation. Thus through the deepening of this sense of basic identity humans participate fully in the transformative aspects of the universe.

The implications of such an understanding relate directly to views of nature and to the cultivation of virtue. In the Neo-Confucian context, they are not two distinct processes. Tu Weiming has suggested how this anthropocosmic understanding differs from a Western anthropocentric viewpoint: "Confucian humanism is . . . fundamentally different from anthropocentrism because it professes the unity of man and Heaven rather than the imposition of the human will on nature. In fact the anthropocentric assumption that man is put on Earth to pursue knowledge and, as knowledge expands, so does man's dominion over Earth is quite different from the Confucian perception of the pursuit of knowledge as an integral part of one's self-cultivation." "The human transformation of nature, therefore," he continues, "means as much an integrative effort to learn to live harmoniously in one's natural environment as a modest attempt to use the environment to sustain basic livelihood. The idea of exploiting nature is rejected because it is incompatible with the Confucian concern for moral self-development."[124]

In developing their moral nature, then, human beings are entering into the processes of change and transformation. Just as the universe manifests this complex pattern of flux and fecundity, so do human beings nurture the seeds of virtue within themselves and participate in the human order in this process of ongoing transformation. This is elaborated by many of the Neo-Confucians and by Ekken in particular through a specific understanding of a correspondence between virtues practiced by humans as having their natural counterpart in cosmic processes. The virtue of humaneness, for example, is seen as the human counterpart of the principle of origination (*yuan*) or fecundity in the universe.

Zhu Xi speaks of humaneness as similar to the spirit of life and growth: "Humaneness as the principle of love is comparable to the root of a tree and the spring of water."[125] Elsewhere he notes, "It is like the will to grow, like the seeds of peaches and apricots."[126] Humaneness is thus like "the vital force of spring,"[127] which blossoms in humans, linking them to Heaven, Earth, and all things: "For humaneness as constituting the Way, consists of the fact that the mind of Heaven and Earth to produce things is present in everything." In his "Treatise on Humaneness," Zhu Xi speaks of the four moral qualities of the mind of Heaven and Earth: origination, flourish, advantage, and firmness (*yuan, heng, li,* and *chen*).[128] These four qualities have also been translated as sublime beginnings, pushing through to success, usefulness that furthers, and firm perseverance. Similarly, in the mind of humans there are four moral qualities: humaneness, rightness, propriety, and wisdom. For many of the Confucians, and for Ekken in particular, the cosmological and the human virtues are seen as part of one dynamic process of transformation in the universe.

The concept of human beings forming a triad with Heaven and Earth and, indeed, affecting the growth and transformation of things through their self-cultivation and their institutions is very old in Confucian thought. As Xunzi wrote in the third century B.C.E., "Heaven has its seasons, Earth has its resources, and man has his government. For this reason it is said that they may form a triad. If one abandons that which allows him to form a triad, yet longs for the triad, he is deluded."[129] In the following century, the Han Confucian scholar Dong Zhongshu wrote: "Heaven, Earth, and humankind are the foundation of all living things. Heaven engenders all living things, Earth nourishes them, and humankind completes them. With filial and brotherly love, Heaven engenders them; with food and clothing Earth nourishes them; and with rites and music, humankind completes them. These three assist one another just as the hands and feet join to complete the body."[130]

This relationship of Heaven, Earth, and humans is characterized as one of parent and child, and central to this metaphor is the notion of humans as children of the universe. The most well-known statement of this idea is found in Zhang Zai's *Western Inscription*, written in the eleventh century:

> Heaven is my father and Earth is my mother, and even such a small creature as I finds an intimate place in their midst.
>
> Therefore that which extends throughout the universe I regard as my body and that which directs the universe I consider as my nature.
>
> All people are my brothers and sisters, and all things are my companions.[131]

He goes on to say:

> Respect the aged. . . . Show affection toward the orphaned and the weak. . . . The sage identifies his character with that of Heaven and Earth, and the worthy is the best [among the children of Heaven and Earth]. Even those who are tired and infirm, crippled or sick, those who have no brothers or children, wives or husbands, are all my brothers who are in distress and who have no one to turn to.[132]

The larger cosmological significance of this important statement has been clearly articulated by Tu Weiming:

> Zhang Zai reminds us that no matter how small a being we find ourselves to be in the vastness of the cosmos, there is not only a lo-

cus but also an intimate place for each of us. For we are all potentially guardians and indeed co-creators of the universe. In this holistic vision of man, an ontological gap between Creator and creature would seem to be almost inconceivable. It appears that there is no post-lapsarian state to encounter and that alienation as a deep-rooted feeling of estrangement from one's primordial origin is nonexistent. Furthermore, the idea of a man as a manipulator and conqueror of nature would also seem to be ruled out.[133]

Ekken expressed this cosmological understanding as a sense of filiality to Heaven and Earth, the Great Parents and the source of all life:

Heaven and Earth give birth to and nourish all things, but the deep compassion with which they treat humans is different from [the way they nourish] birds and beasts, trees and plants. Therefore, among all things only humans are the children of the universe. Thus humans have Heaven as their father and Earth as their mother and receive their great kindness. Because of this, always to serve Heaven and Earth is the Human Way.[134]

The Significance of *Qi* as an Ecological Cosmology

It is clear that Neo-Confucianism may be a rich source for rethinking our own relationship to nature in the light of present ecological concerns.[135] One of the contemporary legacies of the eighteenth-century French Enlightenment is the separation of matter and spirit. A result of this separation is that in the modern period nature has become largely identified as matter that can be manipulated. Consequently, the sense of reverence for nature has been removed and the grounds for exploitation set in place. Nature is seen as a resource simply to be used rather than a source of life that needs to be respected and cared for while still drawing on it for food, clothing, and shelter. This pervasive use mentality is now threatening to unravel the very fabric of the ecosystem on which all life depends. We need new understandings of material reality as not simply a dead, inanimate thing but as something infused with energetic and transformative possibilities inherently connected to humans. Such understandings are present in Confucianism, especially in a figure such as Kaibara Ekken in his philosophy of *qi*.

What motivated Ekken's philosophy of *qi*? Why would such a major intellectual be concerned to explore the profound connection of humans to nature? Why would he devote so much of his life to thinking through the significance of *qi*? Why would he want to record in such intricate detail his respect for Zhu Xi along with his reasons for disagreeing with him regarding *qi*? Why does he affirm Confucius and Mencius in contrast to some of the Song Confucians? Why does he insist again and again that what is at risk is engagement with the world?

Ekken's major preoccupation in the *Record of Great Doubts* is returning to the world, returning to the vitality of things. In making this turn, he is grounded in the fundamental Confucian impulse to cultivate self, society, land, and nature as one continuous stream of energy. Ekken wishes to make visible the constantly renewing power of *qi*, an energy that will not be depleted but rather is perpetually replete with fecund potential. Ekken reaffirms *qi* as primal and primary, for he sees it as an indispensable source of vigor and strength. If humans are to contribute to society and be in right relationship with nature, they have to cultivate *qi*. Otherwise, they become dried-up, rigid, insincere—like the overly cerebral scholars he criticizes. For Ekken vibrancy and joy are necessary for a full and productive life. Thus he feels we need to drink deeply from the wellspring of *qi*.

Yet in all of this there is balance, there is a search for principle within material force. There is the realization in Ekken that one does not just flow aimlessly or recklessly with *qi*; rather one seeks the deeper patterns (*li*) for self-cultivation within and investigation

of things without. There is the need for both discernment to practice virtue and discrimination to explore nature; they are part of a
single continuum of sustained effort. This effort not only is for personal satisfaction or scholarly production, but is generated also to
expand the human mind-and-heart to embrace the larger society,
the natural world, and the universe itself. Thus Ekken aspires to
evoke in humans a comprehensive compassion for all living things,
as had the Neo-Confucians before him.

Ekken realizes that when the vital force of *qi* activates our profound
sense of connection, our attention and concern for all life-forms flow
freely. For Ekken, as for the Confucian tradition at large, *qi* is both
matter and spirit as a unified, vibrant flow. This differentiated yet sin-
gular entity constitutes the very lifeblood of all matter. The *qi* in a tree,
in a stream, in the clouds, and in the grass is part of a vast system of
interacting matter and energy. We dwell amid these luminous pres-
ences and feel their life pulsating in us. Our mutual participation in
qi is not a claim to ownership of one another but a mutual touching of
the depth of things. The tree's branches are ours, their roots are
ours—thus Ekken urges us not to cut down trees wantonly.

This wild world swirling with the vastness and the particularity
of *qi* is part of us and we are part of it. We are born from the con-
junction of these life forces and we rest in the embrace of a universe
that nourishes our life and the life of countless other beings. We
move within the harmony of the ten thousand things and sense the
qi singing throughout.

In entering into this cosmology, reciprocity and reverence arise
effortlessly, and we begin to dance, as Mencius observes, spontane-
ously moving our hands and feet. We cultivate this vibrant *qi*, drawing it in in the morning, breathing it out in the evening, sinking
into it in the depths of night. Restoration and renewal abound in
these rhythms of the day, in the cycles of the season. We are surrounded by this sea of energy, *qi* moving us into the creativity of our

human tasks—building sustainable societies; fostering humane political systems; encouraging the arts of music, poetry, and painting;
cultivating the land; enjoying the fruits of nature; reflecting on the
beauty of the seasons; and reaching toward the stars burning in the
darkness of the night.

These are the things Ekken aspires to activate—humans at home
in the cosmos, humans completing a triad with Heaven and Earth,
and humans restoring filial gratitude to nature for the immense
gifts of life. These are at the heart of his philosophy of *qi*. Not simply
dry argumentation with ancient scholars and obscure texts, Ekken's
vision is rather an impassioned plea for continued contact with the
vital sources of life energy: *qi* in its endless fecundity and mysterious depths; *qi* in its wondrous call to return to the radiance of things,
here now before us displaying the special intricacy and immense
possibilities of change.

For at the heart of *qi* is this profound appreciation for transformation that fascinated the Neo-Confucians. How to be in harmony
with changes in nature, how to be in contact with changes in the
human heart and mind—such are the challenges of cultivating *qi*
within and without. A cultivation for the love of nature; for the pres-
ervation of life; for the hopes of humans; for the shaping of cultures; for the elevation of the human spirit; for the participation in
mutually enhancing human-Earth relations. This is the vision that
Ekken places before us as he invites us across the span of the centuries into the energizing field of vital force.

NOTES

1. Indeed, a conference held in his honor in Fukuoka in April 1994 was
well attended and preceded a major international conference on Confucianism in East Asia. A special library has been established in Fukuoka to collect
all the writings published on Ekken in both Japan and the West. I have chosen
to romanize his name as Ekken, following the practice in Ryusaku Tsunoda,

Wm. Theodore de Bary, and Donald Keene, eds., *Sources of Japanese Tradition* (New York: Columbia University Press, 1958); it is also romanized as Ekiken.

2. My translation of the *Record of Great Doubts* is based on the standard unannotated text in *Ekken zenshū* [*The Collected Works of Kaibara Ekken*], ed. Ekkenkai (Tokyo: Ekken zenshū kankōbu, 1911), 2:149–175, and the annotated text in *Kaibara Ekken, Muro Kyūsō*, ed. Inoue Tadashi and Araki Kengo, Nihon shisō taikei (Tokyo: Iwanami shoten, 1970), 34:10–64 (hereafter cited as NST). The late Professor Okada Takehiko of Kyushu University also made available to me a photocopy of the handwritten version of the original text.

3. On-cho Ng and Kai-wing Chow, "Introduction: Fluidity of the Confucian Canon and Discursive Strategies," in *Imagining Boundaries: Changing Confucian Doctrines, Texts, and Hermeneutics*, ed. Kai-wing Chow, On-cho Ng, and John B. Henderson (Albany: State University of New York Press, 1999), 14.

4. These are collected in volume 3 of *Ekken zenshū*. Four have been translated into English: *Yōjōkun* (*Precepts on Health Care*), *Onna daigaku* (*Learning for Women*), *Rakkun* (*The Way of Contentment*), and *Yamato zokkun* (*Precepts for Daily Life in Japan*). See *Yōjōkun: Japanese Secret of Good Health*, trans. Masao Kunihiro (Tokyo: Tokuma shoten, 1974); "Onna daigaku," trans. Basil Hall Chamberlain, in *Japanese Things* (1905; reprint, Rutland, Vt.: Tuttle, 1971); *The Way of Contentment*, trans. Ken Hoshino (London: John Murray, 1913); and "Yamato zokkun," trans. Mary Evelyn Tucker, in *Moral and Spiritual Cultivation in Japanese Neo-Confucianism: The Life and Thought of Kaibara Ekken, 1630–1714* (Albany: State University of New York Press, 1989).

5. The emergence of a Tokugawa political ideology actually combined elements of Shinto, Buddhism, and Confucianism, as Herman Ooms has demonstrated in *Tokugawa Ideology: Early Constructs, 1570–1680* (Princeton: Princeton University Press, 1985).

6. The major discussion in English of practical learning in the Tokugawa period is in Wm. Theodore de Bary and Irene Bloom, eds., *Principle and Practicality: Essays in Neo-Confucianim and Practical Learning* (New York: Columbia University Press, 1979).

7. Ekken, *Yōjōkun.*

8. This designation was given by the German physician and naturalist Philipp Franz von Siebold (1796–1866), who visited Japan in the nineteenth century. See Ayanori Onishi, "Preface," in Ekken, *Yōjōkun*, 7. On Siebold, see John Bowers, *Western Medical Pioneers in Feudal Japan* (Baltimore: Johns Hopkins University Press, 1970), 91–173.

9. It is important to note that for the Tokugawa period, constituting nearly

three hundred years, there are fewer than twenty Neo-Confucian texts translated into English.

10. "The Doctrine of the Mean," in *A Source Book in Chinese Philosophy*, trans. and comp. Wing-tsit Chan (Princeton: Princeton University Press, 1963), 108.

11. Wm. Theodore de Bary, "Foreword," in Zhu Xi, *Reflections on Things at Hand*, trans. Wing-tsit Chan (New York: Columbia University Press, 1967), vii.

12. Wing-tsit Chan, "Introduction," in ibid., xx.

13. This section and the following on Zhang Zai appear in a slightly different form in Mary Evelyn Tucker, "An Ecological Cosmology: The Confucian Philosophy of Material Force," in *Ecological Prospects: Scientific, Religious, and Aesthetic Perspectives*, ed. Christopher Key Chapple (Albany: State University of New York Press, 1994), 105–126.

14. Wing-tsit Chan, "Appendix: On Translating Certain Chinese Philosophical Terms," in *Source Book*, trans. Chan, 784.

15. Ibid.

16. *Mencius* 2:A2. References here and subsequently are to *Mencius*, trans. D. C. Lau (Harmondsworth: Penguin, 1970).

17. Chan, "Appendix: On Translating," 784.

18. Ibid.

19. *Mencius* 2:A2.

20. Quoted in Huang Siu-chi, "Chang Tsai's Concept of *Ch'i*," *Philosophy East and West* 18, no. 4 (1968): 251. I am indebted to Huang's article for some of the ideas in this first paragraph.

21. Tang Chūn-I (Tang Junyi), "Chang Tsai's Theory of Mind," *Philosophy East and West* 6, no. 2 (1956): 121.

22. Zhang Zai, "Correcting Youthful Ignorance," trans. Wing-tsit Chan, in *Sources of Chinese Tradition*, ed. Wm. Theodore de Bary and Irene Bloom (New York: Columbia University Press, 1999), 1:685.

23. Tang, "Chang Tsai's Theory of Mind," 123.

24. Fung Yu-lan, *A Short History of Chinese Philosophy* (New York: Free Press, 1948), 280.

25. Zhang Zai, "Correcting Youthful Ignorance," 503.

26. Ibid.

27. Quoted in Huang, "Chang Tsai's Concept of *Ch'i*," 253.

28. Tang is using the process philosopher Alfred North Whitehead's term here ("Chang Tsai's Theory of Mind," 123–125).

29. Ibid., 124.

30. Ibid., 125.
31. Ibid., 127.
32. Ibid., 126.
33. Zhang Zai, "Correcting Youthful Ignorance," 505.
34. Ibid., 497.
35. Ibid., 497–498.
36. This is a phrase used by Thomas Berry to describe the spiritual dimension of the Confucian tradition, in "Individualism and Holism in Chinese Tradition: The Religious Cultural Context," in *Confucian Spirituality*, ed. Tu Weiming and Mary Evelyn Tucker (New York: Crossroad, 2003), 1:50.
37. Zhang Zai, "Correcting Youthful Ignorance," 505.
38. Ibid., 513. For a clarification of Zhang Zai's doctrine of evil, I am indebted to Chan's comments in his *Source Book* and in his "The Neo-Confucian Solution to the Problem of Evil," in *Neo-Confucianism, Etc.: Essays by Wing-tsit Chan*, comp. Charles K. H. Chen (Hanover, N.H.: Oriental Society, 1969).
39. Chan, "Neo-Confucian Solution," 102.
40. Luo Qinshun, *Knowledge Painfully Acquired: The K'un-chih chi by Lo Ch'in-shun*, trans. Irene Bloom (New York: Columbia University Press, 1987).
41. Abe Yoshio, *Nihon Shushigaku to Chōsen [The Japanese Zhu Xi School and Korea]* (Tokyo: Tokyo Daigaku shuppankai, 1971), 494–497.
42. Young-chan Ro, *The Korean Neo-Confucianism of Yi Yulgok* (Albany: State University of New York Press, 1989).
43. It is interesting to note, however, that the primary influence on Ekken appears to have been Luo Qinshun, not Yi Yulgok.
44. Luo, *Knowledge Painfully Acquired*, 58.
45. Ibid.
46. Ibid., 109.
47. Ibid., 127
48. Ibid., 134.
49. Ibid., 84.
50. Ibid., 161–162.
51. Ibid., 65.
52. Ibid.
53. Irene Bloom, "Introduction," in ibid., 23.
54. Ng and Chow, "Introduction," 2.
55. C. R. Boxer, *The Christian Century in Japan, 1549–1650* (Berkeley: University of California Press, 1951); George Elison, *Deus Destroyed: The Image of*

Christianity in Early Modern Japan (Cambridge, Mass.: Harvard University Press, 1973).

56. Ronald Toby, *State and Diplomacy in Early Modern Japan: Asia in the Development of the Tokugawa Bakufu* (Princeton: Princeton University Press, 1984); Bob Tadashi Wakabayashi, *Anti-Foreignism and Western Learning in Early-Modern Japan* (Cambridge, Mass.: Harvard University Press, 1986). Wakabayashi argues that the Japanese isolation from trade with other countries was due more to the Dutch desire to control trade in East Asia and their reluctance to share it with the Japanese.

57. Books with references to Christianity were proscribed, but books on Western science, especially medicine and astronomy, were imported at will. These became the basis for the flourishing field of Dutch studies (*rangaku*).

58. For a detailed study of the changing role of the samurai in the Tokugawa period, see Eiko Ikegami, *The Taming of the Samurai: Honorific Individualism and the Making of Modern Japan* (Cambridge, Mass.: Harvard University Press, 1995).

59. Tetsuo Najita, *Visions of Virtue in Tokugawa Japan: The Kaitokudō Merchant Academy of Osaka* (Chicago: University of Chicago Press, 1987).

60. Peter Nosco, "Introduction," in *Confucianism and Tokugawa Culture*, ed. Peter Nosco (Princeton: Princeton University Press, 1984), 26.

61. Najita, *Visions of Virtue*, 60–61.

62. Ian James McMullen, *Idealism, Protest and "The Tale of Genji": The Confucianism of Kumazawa Banzan* (Oxford: Clarendon Press, 1999).

63. Olof Lidin, *The Life of Ogyū Sorai, a Tokugawa Confucian Philosopher* (Lund: Scandinavian Institute of Asian Studies, 1973); *Ogyū Sorai's "Distinguishing the Way,"* trans. Olof Lidin (Tokyo: Sophia University Press, 1970); *Master Sorai's Responsals: An Annotated Translation of "Sorai sensei tōmonsho,"* trans. Samuel H. Yamashita (Honolulu: University of Hawaii Press, 1994); John A. Tucker, *Itō Jinsai's "Gomō Jigi" and the Philosophical Definition of Early Modern Japan* (Leiden: Brill, 1998).

64. Kate Nakai, "The Naturalization of Confucianism in Tokugawa Japan: The Problem of Sinocentrism," *Harvard Journal of Asian Studies* 40 (1980): 157–199.

65. Tetsuo Najita discusses this in relation to Ekken in "Intellectual Change in Early Eighteenth-Century Tokugawa Confucianism," *Journal of Asian Studies* 34, no. 4 (1975): 931–944.

66. "Kinshiroku bikō," in *Ekken zenshū*, 2:637. Ekken cites Xue Xuan in the *Dushu lu* (*Record of My Reading*).

67. Okada Takehiko, "Practical Learning in the Chu Hsi School: Yamazaki Ansai and Kaibara Ekken," in *Principle and Practicality*, ed. de Bary and Bloom, 264.

68. Ibid., 267.

69. Ogyū Sorai to Takeda Shun'an, in *Ekken shiryō* 6:69, quoted in ibid., 263.

70. Postface to Ekken, *Taigiroku*, quoted in ibid.

71. Ibid., 290. The careful effort to avoid or to identify "heresy" is discussed in John B. Henderson, "Strategies in Neo-Confucian Heresiography," in *Imagining Boundaries*, ed. Chow, Ng, and Henderson, 107–120.

72. Michael Kalton, Oaksoot C. Kim, and Sung Bae Park, *The Four-Seven Debate: An Annotated Translation of the Most Famous Controversy in Korean Neo-Confucian Thought* (Albany: State University of New York Press, 1994), xvii.

73. For a translation of this intricate and prolonged debate, see ibid.

74. Wm. Theodore de Bary has discussed Confucian learning in various volumes, especially *Learning for Oneself: Essays on the Individual in Neo-Confucian Thought* (New York: Columbia University Press, 1991). See also David Hall and Roger Ames, *Thinking Through Confucius* (Albany: State University of New York Press, 1987).

75. De Bary, *Learning for Oneself*, 8.

76. Indeed, de Bary suggests that "there has probably been no other tradition so clearly committed to scholarship as Confucianism" (ibid., 54).

77. Ibid., 43.

78. Ekken, *Taigiroku*, NST, 1.

79. Ibid.

80. Ibid., 37, 41.

81. *Analects* 1:1.

82. "Doctrine of the Mean," in *Source Book*, trans. Chan, 110.

83. Ekken, *Taigiroku*, NST, 78.

84. Zhou Dunyi, "Explanation of the Diagram of the Supreme Polarity" (*Taiji tushuo*), in *Sources of Chinese Tradition*, ed. de Bary and Bloom, 1:672–676.

85. Ekken, *Taigiroku*, NST, 52.

86. Okada, "Practical Learning in the Chu Hsi School," 287.

87. Chou Tun-i (Zhou Dunyi), "An Explanation of the Diagram of the Great Ultimate," in *Source Book*, trans. Chan, 463.

88. Zhu Xi, *Reflections on Things at Hand*, 5.

89. De Bary, *Learning for Oneself*, 74.

90. Ibid., 91.

91. Ekken, *Taigiroku*, NST, 52. Chan indicates, however, that he was not able to locate the term *wuji* in the Buddhist text (Zhu Xi, *Reflections on Things at Hand*, 5n.2).

92. Ekken, *Taigiroku*, NST, 62.

93. Ibid., 61.

94. Ibid., 62.

95. Luo, *Knowledge Painfully Acquired*, 173.

96. Zhu Xi, "Principle and Material-Force," in *Sources of Chinese Tradition*, ed. de Bary and Bloom, 1:701.

97. *Mencius* 2A:6.

98. "Rakkun," in *Ekken zenshū*, 3:605.

99. Itō Tomonobu, ed., *Shinshiroku* [*Record of Careful Thoughts*] (Tokyo: Kōdansha, 1966), 52, 53, 100, 128.

100. Ekken, "Rakkun," 3:631.

101. *Yōjōkun*, in *Ekken zenshū*, 3:86, quoted in Okada, "Practical Learning in the Chu Hsi School," 283.

102. For a discussion of this process, see Chow, Ng, and Henderson, eds., *Imagining Boundaries*.

103. Minamoto Ryōen, "*Jitsugaku* and Empirical Rationalism in the First Half of the Tokugawa Period," in *Principle and Practicality*, ed. de Bary and Bloom, 375–470.

104. Minamoto Ryōen, *Tokugawa gōri shisō no keifu* [*The Lineage of Rational Thought in the Tokugawa Period*] (Tokyo: Chūō kōronsha, 1972), and *Kinsei shoki jitsugaku shisō no kenkyū* [*Studies in Practical Learning at the Beginning of the Premodern Era*] (Tokyo: Sōbunsha, 1980).

105. Ronald P. Dore, *Education in Tokugawa Japan* (Berkeley: University of California Press, 1965); Richard Rubinger, *Private Academies of Tokugawa Japan* (Princeton: Princeton University Press, 1982). The early study of the modernization of Japan was led by Marius Jansen. See, for example, Marius Jansen, ed., *Changing Japanese Attitudes Toward Modernization* (Princeton: Princeton University Press, 1965).

106. Masao Maruyama, *Studies in the Intellectual History of Tokugawa Japan*, trans. Mikiso Hane (Princeton: Princeton University Press, 1974).

107. The section that follows draws on my discussion in "Introduction," in *Moral and Spiritual Cultivation*.

108. Okada, "Practical Learning in the Chu Hsi School," 268.

109. Ibid., 279.

110. Ibid., 277.

111. Ibid., 257–258.

112. Maruyama, *Intellectual History of Tokugawa Japan*. See also Robert Bellah, "Notes on Maruyama Masao," in *Imagining Japan: The Japanese Tradition and Its Modern Interpretation* (Berkeley: University of California Press, 2003), 140–149.

113. Abe, *Nihon Shushigaku to Chōsen*.

114. As Tu Weiming notes, the philosophers of *qi* cannot be seen as only materialistic. Rather, for them *qi* "was not simply matter but vital force endowed with all-pervasive spirituality" ("The Continuity of Being: Chinese Visions of Nature," in *Confucian Thought: Selfhood as Creative Transformation* [Albany: State University of New York Press, 1985], 37).

115. Najita, "Intellectual Change," 933.

116. Ibid., 935.

117. Ibid., 936.

118. Ibid., 940.

119. Najita, *Visions of Virtue*, 47.

120. Tu Weiming, "The Continuity of Being: Chinese Visions of Nature," in *Nature in Asian Traditions of Thought*, ed. J. Baird Callicott and Roger Ames (Albany: State University of New York Press, 1989), 67–78.

121. Wang Fu-Chih (Wang Fuzhi), "Unceasing Growth and Man's Nature and Destiny," in *Source Book*, trans. Chan, 698.

122. Tu, "Continuity of Being," 70.

123. Tu, *Confucian Thought*.

124. Tu Weiming, "The Value of the Human in Classical Confucian Thought," in ibid., 75.

125. *Zhuzi quanshu* 47:37a, quoted in Wing-tsit Chan, "The Concept of Man in Chinese Thought," in *Neo-Confucianism*, comp. Chen, 155.

126. Ibid.

127. Zhu Xi, "A Treatise on *Jen*," in *Source Book*, trans. Chan, 594.

128. Ibid.

129. *Xunzi*, in *Sources of Chinese Tradition*, ed. de Bary and Bloom, 1:171.

130. Dong Zhongshu, "Establishing the Primal Numen," in ibid., 299.

131. Zhang Zai, "The 'Western Inscription,'" in ibid., 683.

132. Ibid.

133. Tu Weiming, "Neo-Confucian Ontology: A Preliminary Questioning," in *Confucian Thought*, 158.

134. "Yamato zokkun," in *Ekken zenshū*, 3:47, trans. in Tucker, *Moral and Spiritual Cultivation*, 136.

135. See, for example, Mary Evelyn Tucker and John Berthrong, eds., *Confucianism and Ecology: The Interrelation of Heaven, Earth, and Humans* (Cambridge, Mass.: Center for the Study of World Religions and Harvard University Press, 1998).

TAIGIROKU

The *Record of Great Doubts*

An earlier Confucian[1] said, "In learning it is regrettable if we do not have doubts. If we doubt there will be advancement and consequently we will learn. Beginning students cannot understand every aspect of what they study. Accordingly, it is essential to have doubts in pursuing the way of learning. Indeed, doubts should be respected, for without them one won't make progress."[2] As Zhu Xi said, "It is important for those who do not usually doubt to have doubts, and it is necessary for those who have doubts to resolve them."[3] He also noted that "if our doubt is great, our progress will be significant; if our doubt is small, our progress will be insignificant. If we don't have doubts we won't progress."[4]

In my humble opinion, after one studies one begins to doubt; after one doubts one starts to raise questions; after one questions one begins to reflect; and after one reflects one finally understands. The way of learning should follow this pattern. For example, the learning process can be compared to walking down a road. If we walk for a while without stopping, we will inevitably come to a point where the road divides and we won't know which way to go. At this point we will have doubts and, being confused, we will be unable to proceed. Thus, we must ask for directions. Yet if we don't walk on the path, how will we have doubts? Presumably, it is because we proceed along the road without stopping that we have doubts and questions. Indeed, for this reason the ancient scholars combined the idea of learning and questioning.[5]

From the age of fourteen or fifteen, I set my mind on the learning of the sages.[6] From my youth I have read the books of the Song Confucians and have devoted myself to their teachings. For a long time I took them as the greatest models. I have also had great doubts but, lacking sufficient understanding, I have not been able to dispel them, nor did I have an enlightened teacher whom I could question. Now, as I have become older, I have even less ability to resolve my perplexities. For more than thirty years I have continued to ponder deeply, but it is my greatest regret that I still harbor doubts within myself and cannot fully comprehend certain teachings. For the present I will describe my misgivings here in the hope of being enlightened by more knowledgeable scholars. How can I possibly claim that my ideas alone are correct and defend my own views against those of scholars of earlier generations?

Chikuzen [Fukuoka], Shotoku (1713), vernal equinox
Kaibara Atsunobu, eighty-four years old

PART I

On the Transmission of Confucian Thought

1

Although in great antiquity there were people who received Heaven's will and established the basis of moral principles, the method of instruction regarding the Way of the sages was not made known. From the time of Yao and Shun,[7] people were urged to "be refined and single-minded, holding fast to the Mean"[8] and to "reverently spread the teachings of the five constant virtues."[9] This may be considered the beginning of the establishment of education. The three periods of the Xia, Shang, and Zhou[10] followed and gradually this educational method was refined. However, it was not yet clearly articulated. Confucius greatly clarified it. The Way of Confucius was accurately transmitted to Mencius, who expounded it with clarity.

From ancient times the revolving energies of Heaven and Earth have gradually changed over time. The unfolding of human civilization has also followed these changes unceasingly. Even in the enlightened period of Yao and Shun and the three early dynasties civilization was unable to flower fully, and thus it is natural that further developments awaited later generations. Indeed, for the many generations to come, civilization will gradually yet ceaselessly unfold with each age.

After Mencius, from the Han through the Tang periods,[11] the transmission of the Way was nearly cut off. Indeed, it shrank to a slender thread. However, in the Song dynasty several exemplary teachers appeared who resuscitated the Way and it again became prominent.[12] Particularly noteworthy were the commentaries and the explanations of the Confucian classics by the Cheng brothers and Zhu Xi. Since Mencius there have been many remarkable scholars, but the Cheng brothers were the most illustrious among those who knew the Way and explicated the teachings. After them was Zhu Xi. However, neither their virtue nor their learning were comparable to that attained by the earlier sages. Later generations naturally respected and trusted the Cheng brothers and Zhu Xi, but in their teachings there may be various points that are not in agreement with Confucius and Mencius. Therefore, we must not regard the Song Confucians as equal to Confucius and Mencius. Scholars should have an open mind and be discerning with regard to the similarities and differences, and the correctness and mistakes of their teachings. Moreover, they should reflect deeply, select carefully, and then believe what they should believe and doubt what they should doubt. If they do this, everything will be fine.

An ancient scholar said, "To learn is to understand; it is to realize what we don't know [fully]."[13] Accordingly, the way of learning is to resolve doubts and dispel misgivings. In learning we regard the ability to doubt as brilliance; the inability to doubt as dullness. In this spirit, Zhu Xi said, "If our doubt is great, our progress will be significant; if our doubt is small, our progress will be insignificant. If we don't have doubts we won't progress."[14]

However, even in doubting there is a right and a wrong way. Our doubt is correct when, upon careful reflection, it is unavoidable. To doubt indiscriminately is to diffuse one's efforts into unimportant things, and this should not be considered appropriate.

2

In their teachings, the Song Confucians regarded the basis of the Supreme Ultimate [*taiji*] to be the infinite or nonfinite [*wuji*].[15] Thus nonfinite was regarded as the root of being. They divided principle (*li*) and material force (*qi*)[16] and regarded them as two things. They did not consider yin and yang as the Way but as physical entities.[17] They divided the nature of Heaven and Earth from physical nature,[18] and they viewed human nature and principle as being without birth and death.[19] These are ideas derived from Buddhism and Daoism; the teachings of the early Confucian sages are different. Scholars must distinguish this precisely and clearly.

In discussing the method of preserving the mind-and-heart [*shin*] the Song Confucians spoke of making tranquility central,[20] of quiet sitting[21] and of understanding the principle of Heaven through silent sitting to purify the mind-and-heart. They regarded quiet sitting to be a daily method for preserving the heart. This all tends toward quietism and implies that activity and tranquility are not in proper accord with circumstances [in balance].[22] In other words, these practices are the same as the techniques of Chan meditation. True Confucians should not promote these views. Song Confucians also spoke of the original mind-and-heart as being unobstructed and clear,[23] and they regarded Heavenly principle as being vast and without traces.[24] These are the ideas of the Buddhists or Daoists; the teachings of Confucius and Mencius are different. The teachings of the Song Confucians generally elaborated on Confucius and Mencius. There are also aspects of their teachings, however, that emerged from Buddhist and Daoist thought and which do not originate with Confucius and Mencius. Scholars must be selective. Song Confu-

cians were definitely forceful in their rejection of Buddhist and Daoist thought, but nonetheless, why did they use paths outside the orthodox way to explain their teachings? The foregoing comments
arise from doubts I have been unable to resolve.

3

I do not know how many books have arisen since the Qin[25] and
Han, but among them there are certainly too many good books to
enumerate. However, the works of Zhu Xi are incomparable in their
vast benefit to scholars. This is because the moral principles in them
are pure and uncorrupted, and there is a range of knowledge with
clarity and breadth. It is rare not to be able to discern the principles
of Heaven and Earth in these works. It is like entering a large shop
to look for something one needs and finding it easily. We are fortunate to be born after Zhu Xi. We can examine his writings and we
should acknowledge that this is a supreme blessing and boundless
good fortune. Because of this, I also respect these writings like gods,
and I rely on them like oracles.

4

After Confucius the only person who attained the highest level in
transmitting the teachings of the sages was Mencius. This is due to
three fortunate conditions. First, Mencius was very talented; second, he lived close to the time of Confucius; and third, he lived his
life in places near where Confucius resided. After Mencius, Zhou
Dunyi, the Cheng brothers, Zhang Zai, and Sima Guang were all
wise men who contributed to the Way of the sages. But among
these, what was transmitted by the Cheng brothers and Zhu Xi was
the soundest. Their learning, compared to that of other Confucian
scholars, was especially broad and refined and naturally became a

model for subsequent scholarship. Consequently, after Mencius the accomplishments of the Cheng brothers and Zhu Xi were significant and, in particular, the achievements of Zhu Xi were of the highest order. Therefore, since the time of Confucius and Mencius, only the Cheng brothers and Zhu Xi can be regarded as truly knowing the Way, and they should be seen as models of learning.

5

In his epilogue to Zhu Xi's *Original Meaning of the Classic of Changes*,[26] Lu Fangweng wrote: "The Way [of Heaven and Earth] spoken of in the *Classic of Changes* is vast and no one person can exhaust it. Thus it is not advisable to adhere stubbornly to a single school of thought."[27] These words of Lu can be said to have clearly explained the attitude of the ancients toward learning.

6

Those who study should not believe only in their own opinions; they should ardently trust their teacher. This is most appropriate. Most people are not sages, and, no matter how intelligent they may be, they are rarely without faults, such as being biased or lacking discrimination. Even the brightness of the sun and the moon can be hidden by clouds; even pearls with the greatest luster may have flaws. In the same way, even among wide-ranging explanations by intelligent people, inevitably some are biased and not completely correct. Therefore, we must be discriminating and believe what we think we should believe and doubt what we think we should doubt. In this way we can select what is good.[28] After we choose the good and have no more doubts, we should hold fast to it. If we wish to hold on to something but do not choose the good, inevitably we cannot avoid being opinionated or biased.

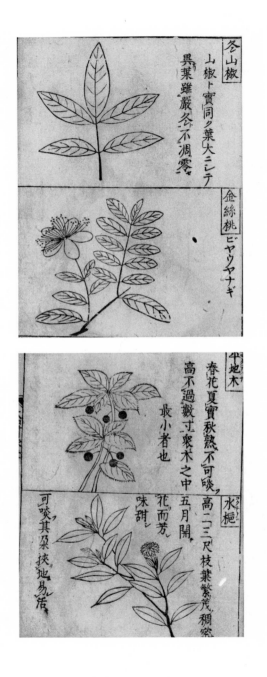

冬山椒

山椒ト實同ク葉大ニシテ
異葉雖嚴冬不凋零

金絲桃
ビヤウヤナギ

千地木

春花夏實秋熟不可啖高二三尺枝葉繁茂稠密
高不過數寸衆木之中五月開
花而芳
最小者也

水梔

可啖其朶挾地易活
味甜

Between Heaven and Earth principle alone is vast and boundless. Thus, one person, no matter how brilliant, cannot comprehend it completely. Therefore, ancient scholars even listened to street gossip or adopted the words of madmen and conversed with woodcutters. They sought knowledge widely in the hope of abiding in the highest good.[29] Because of that even such a wise man as Shun loved to question and investigate everyday expressions. He abandoned his own egotistical views and followed others, questioning and observing widely.[30] The sage had an unselfish and impartial mind but feared that learning could be impeded by relying solely on his own wisdom.

In the *Art of Rulership* it says, "With similar viewpoints, things will not be complete. By approaching things from different perspectives, inevitably people can complete something."[31] Liu Liang, a scholar of the later Han period, said: "There are cases where, although one transgresses, one attains the Way, and there are cases where, even though one is compliant, one loses moral principles."[32] That is the reason that the true person loves honest speech. That is quite different from saying, "Since our paths are different, we don't discuss things together."[33] What I call different is the saying "Although the path to proceed is different, one arrives at the same place."[34] Thus, it is not the same as heretical learning, which reaches a different conclusion.

7

From my youth I have read Zhu Xi's writings. I respected his way, followed his model, and devoted myself to his teachings. However, with regard to unclear points, I have analyzed them thoroughly, but I have never followed the fashion of the times. Nonetheless, I hope for a resolution at some future time.

8

The sages composed the Six Classics.[35] Their writings have been a model throughout the ages; they were trusted and not doubted. The *Classic of Changes*, in particular, is a book that is the pinnacle of refinement. It contains the inner mysteries of the Six Classics and has been a guide for numerous generations. If it is not to be trusted, what can be trusted?

9

"The Way and yin and yang are the same."[36] Before both yin and yang, there is the Chinese character for "one," which refers to the movement and tranquility of the original material force; one is yin and one is yang and there is continual alternation. This alternating flow of yin and yang is ceaseless and mysterious. In my view, the fact that the sages inserted the character for "one" before both yin and yang certainly must have a special significance. Although they didn't add the two characters for "source" [causality],[37] the meaning was sufficient as it was. The words of the sages have been relied on throughout the ages; they should not be doubted. This one phrase in the *Classic of Changes* outlines the foundation for the moral principles of all things. It is improbable that there could be even a single missing character. Why did the later Confucians think some characters were missing and add two characters meaning "source" [causality]? No doubt this was rash; the characters were superfluous (like drawing legs on a snake).

10

The Way constitutes the flow of yin and yang, which is pure and correct; it is the nature of yin and yang, which is not obscured or disordered. As for principle, it is inherent in material force; principle and material force should not be divided into two things.[38] There is no temporal connection of before and after between them.[39] There is no spatial relationship of separation or combination. Thus I think that principle and material force are definitely one entity. Zhu Xi regarded these as two things; this is why I am puzzled and unconvinced.

11

The sages said in another passage in the *Classic of Changes* that yin and yang are the Way.[40] The words of the sages referring to oneness should be trusted throughout the ages and ought not to be doubted. How much more so when the sages repeatedly instruct us on this?

On Human Nature

12

Zhu Xi observed, "The physical body has life and death; but human nature does not."[41] Yi T'oegye, in his *Record of Self-Reflections*, states, "Material force has life and death, but principle has no life and death."[42] With the wisdom of Zhu Xi and with the scholarship of Yi T'oegye, one would not expect these teachings to be inaccurate. However, a foolish person like myself still cannot fathom them. Awaiting the clarification of wiser men, I will elaborate my doubts below and set forth my reflections. My only purpose in doing this is that I hope to be guided by those who possess the Way.[43]

In my view, the body has life if material force is unified; if it disperses, the body dies. Human nature is the principle of life that we receive from Heaven. Principle is inherent in material force; principle and material force are not two separate things. When the body dies, where does the principle of life go? The human body has material force as its basis, and principle is the essence of material force.

Thus if one is living, one has principle; if one dies, principle also disappears.[44] Therefore, it is not logical that when a person dies, human nature lives. If we have a body, there is a human nature; if we don't have a body, this nature also disappears. It has no place to lodge. For example, water and fire are inherently cold and hot or damp and dry, but if water and fire are already extinguished, those attributes of cold and heat, dampness and dryness are also extinguished. Then how can any such attribute survive separately?

13

To say, "Human nature is principle"[45] is not a correct explanation of the character of human nature. The *Doctrine of the Mean* states, "Human nature is what is mandated from Heaven."[46] This means that humans receive a Heavenly destiny, and this is called "human nature." With regard to the character of human nature, this explanation is correct and sufficient without resorting to another. Mencius says, "Our body and complexion are given to us by Heaven."[47] This passage refers to human nature as the physical endowment we have innately received. In the explanations of nature by Confucius, Zisi,[48] and Mencius the meaning is similar. Namely, they speak of human nature as being innately received, and suggest there is no nature other than what is innately received. When Mencius speaks of human nature as good, his words refer to the original nature we receive. This is a unified principle that runs through everything. Some have argued that "there were extremely evil people such as King Jie[49] and King Zhou.[50] There were also people who killed their fathers or their lords, and individuals such as Zi Yue,[51] who was born with the voice of a wild beast. If we evaluate these characteristics from the point of view of physical nature, generally we can't say they have innate goodness.[52] How can we say that all human nature is the same?"[53]

My reply is that "men such as King Jie, King Zhou, and Emperor Yang[54] of the Sui dynasty undoubtedly had evil natures. However, in the principle of the universe there is constancy and there is change. The good is the constancy of human nature; evil is a deviation of human nature. There are very few who deviate and we don't call them normal. To have an evil nature means something is amiss. Hence, it is not wrong to assume that human nature is good. People whose nature is bad, such as King Jie and King Zhou, are probably only one in a million. We can't regard them as the standard.

When we think of the eating and drinking habits of people, it is the usual characteristic of human nature to like sweet things and dislike bitter things. However, among a vast number of people there are a few who will like bitter things and dislike sweet things. We should not regard these people as normal. Those whose natures are evil are similar. Accordingly, human beings in ancient and modern times, whether wise or foolish, should be regarded as good since their natures are similar.

14

Luo Qinshun set forth the theory "Principle is one; its particularizations are many."[55] It is brief, but gets to the point. In it he clearly explained the character of human nature. Therefore, we don't need to analyze it in great detail. In my opinion, human nature is simply one. We can't divide nature into the nature of Heaven and Earth and the physical disposition. "Principle is one" means the original nature has one principle and is equally good. The variations of human nature are equivalent to "the particularizations are many." Anyone can become a Yao or Shun.[56] "Particularizations are many" refers to the fact that the physical disposition (by which one receives the two material forces of yin and yang) is different in each person.

It is said that "by nature humans are alike, but through practice they differ."[57] Thus, "only the wisest and the most ignorant do not change."[58] Physical disposition is the root meaning of human nature; it is what one receives from Heaven. The nature of Heaven and

Earth is also one's received innate nature. This does not mean, however, that two natures exist. Therefore, because there were cases where they were called by two names, there were some doubts as to whether two natures existed. No other way of explaining human nature is better than explaining it as: "Principle is one; its particularizations are many," which is easy to understand and so does not raise doubts. In my opinion, the original state of human nature is the original physical disposition and is decreed from Heaven. There are not two natures. For example, in water the current, the overflow, and the moistness are all characteristics of water. The purity of water is its original form. The characteristics and the original form are not two separate things.

On Bias, Discernment, and Selection

15

In ancient times to the present there has been only one Confucius in the world. Boyi[59] and Liuxia Hui [60] had exceptional virtue and superior constancy and harmony. Yet they were not without faults such as narrowness and a lack of dignity, respectively.[61] Thus they can't be compared to Confucius. This is even more true of those who are not equal in virtue to Boyi or Liu. The comparison between the Song Confucians and Confucius is the same. They are said to have followed the sages and opened the way to future learning.[62] But they were also biased and stubborn and could not always discern appropriate differences of meaning. As a result, it is natural that their explanations sometimes differ from the words of the sages. Although the Cheng brothers and Zhu Xi had an insightful philosophy, how can they be ranked with Confucius? Therefore, in reading the Song Confucians, scholars should know what to adopt or reject among their explanations.

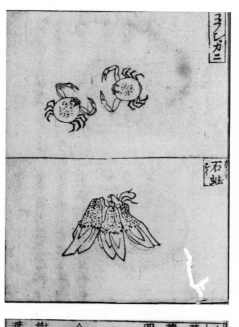

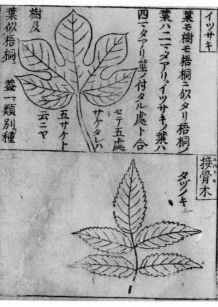

ユビレガニ

石蛆

イツサキ

葉モ樹モ梧桐ニ似タリ梧桐ノ
葉ハ二ニマタアリ・イツサキノ葉ハ
四ニマタアリ莖ノ付タル處ト合
セテ五處
サケタレハ
五サケト
云ニヤ
樹及
葉似梧桐　盖一類別種

接骨木

タヅノキ

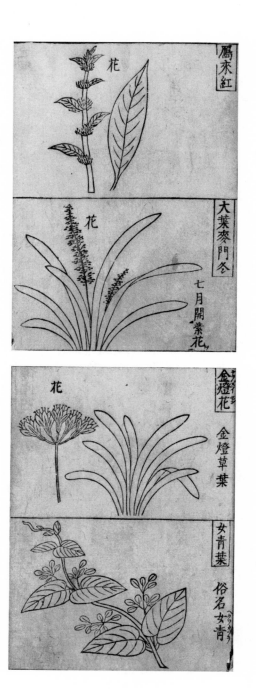

鴈來紅　花

大葉麥門冬　花　七月開紫花

金燈花　金燈草葉　花

女青葉　俗名女青

16

People are not sages and, even if they are wise, they often have biases. In both scholarship and disposition certainly they may have discernment or they may be impeded in their understanding. Therefore, they will have strong points and weak points. What is understood will definitely become clear, but what is blocked definitely stagnates. Consequently, in reading books, even those of wise people, we must be discriminating in our selection. If we are biased and credulous, and without any doubts, probably we can't avoid falling into the errors resulting from obstinacy and confusion. When scholars question the thought of the earlier Confucians, they should believe what is trustworthy and doubt what is suspicious. If they are impartial and not prejudiced in their selections, they can do scholarly work well. Scholars of later ages frequently followed the fashionable school of the day and thus are often guilty of narrowness and obstinacy.

17

In my opinion, the ideas of the Supreme Ultimate, yin and yang, the Way [formless] and concrete things [forms], principle, material force, the mind-and-heart, and human nature have one origin from ages past. Numerous sages have followed this one path and have penetrated to a common understanding of the Five Classics and the Four Books. This is the reason from past to present they had common premises for their ideas that perpetuated the Way. After Mencius, through the Han and Tang and down to recent times,[63] people who avidly pursued only the new learning[64] and lost sight of the classical learning[65] sometimes had differences with the ancient sage-kings.

Even though they were remarkable scholars, it was inevitable that they would have biases and errors. Students ought to pick and choose carefully [in reading their works]. In my opinion, there are wise people who claim certain ideas to be the Way even though the sages did not mention them. These are the implied meanings of the explanations of the sages, which have continued from past to present. However, teachings different from the essential doctrines of the sages ought to be considered heterodox. Therefore, even though they are the words of wise people, we ought to be selective and investigate them if there are some that are not the same as the sages' teachings.

18

When the late Ming Confucians rejected the teachings of the Song Confucians,[66] they were frequently overbearing and self-confident. They looked down on the Cheng brothers and Zhu Xi as if they were inferior. Furthermore, they claimed Song learning was heterodox and not orthodox. Indeed, they saw themselves as superior and lost sight of their own position.

If we compare this [attitude] to [our approach] when we admonish people, we should be restrained and not speak too sharply. If we think it is appropriate to abuse and slander people and reveal their faults,[67] and if we exaggerate their small mistakes, this is extremely rude. Even though there may be some truth in what we say, those who hear this type of criticism will resent it and not accept it. On the contrary, they will resist it and will not change. This is not knowing the [appropriate] way to admonish people.

The later [Ming] Confucians criticized the Song Confucians in a similar manner. They didn't know how to speak of these things. How many instances there are where their words are unreasonable! This shows that criticizing is easy but speaking tactfully is difficult.

19

In general, debating the truth and falsity of scholarship with people is the same as admonishing others. Those who criticize others rashly want to promote their own ideas and humiliate others. Such methods are used by petty individuals who persistently try to outdo other people, thinking they are right and acting in an indiscreet, proud manner. This is not the Way of the true person, which involves sincerity and sympathy. Although there may be some truth in their opinions, if a person is belligerent the listener won't be persuaded. Those who lead people skillfully place priority on intentions. Since their manner of speaking is tolerant and not aggressive, while their expression is suggestive and composed and their meaning is clear, the listener will be convinced and will heed their words. This is an effective way of giving sincere advice.

When one is discussing differences of opinion with others, there is no need to be vehemently antagonistic. When we are calm and suggestive and when we are sincere and moderate in speech, people will indeed be moved. In my opinion, if people are not honest, the Way will be obscured. However, one should not forcefully disparage others' faults. We should only hope for truth to prevail. We should not argue, desiring that our own opinions dominate others. Moreover, if our words are indiscreet, and we try to win and outperform others, we won't convince them. On the contrary, we may cause antagonism. As Confucius said, "To speak with those who cannot be spoken to is to waste one's words."[68] In the words of Xu Weichang,[69] "The true person doesn't speak when he doesn't have a suitable opponent."[70] In *Conversations of the States* it says, "Only the good person is able to receive frank suggestions."[71] Thus, we should speak only with good people. If we speak with others, it will be a waste of words.

20

"The sage is a teacher to a hundred generations."[72] Mencius was a Confucian of great achievement because he faithfully followed the Way of Confucius without straying. Among the teachings of the Song scholars, those that follow the teachings of Confucius and

Mencius faithfully, having the same source and penetrating to a similar truth, those teachings truly illuminate the Way, and, thus, we should rely on them. However, frequently discussions occur that propose a different argument not based on the teachings of Confucius and Mencius and which do not have the same source or school of thought. Even if they are the words of wise people, we should not accept them.

21

"It is by weighing a thing that its weight can be known and by measuring it that its length can be ascertained."[73] Those who want to know the strong and weak points of scholarship should do exactly this. Between sages and worthies there are fundamental differences. Even if people use the words of earlier Confucians, when they aren't consistent with shared moral principles, we shouldn't accept them unconditionally. Having a standard in mind to follow, we should determine the differences between things.

Thus, although the Song Confucians are wise philosophers, they are not in the same category as the sages, and there are bound to be discrepancies. From the end of the Song through the Yuan and Ming, men of inferior scholarship frequently flattered Zhu Xi and differed with the sages. They are said to have had no standard to follow. Why did it become a custom that the Confucians of later ages flatter Zhu Xi and follow him blindly? Can we say they are studying Zhu Xi carefully?

22

Scholars after the Song respected the Cheng brothers and Zhu Xi and naturally that was good, but obstinate ones didn't know the distinction between the sage and the worthy. Because they were not able to discern the differences, they came to regard the ideas of the

Song Confucians as identical with the words of the sages. Although this was contrary to moral principles, they were not troubled by it; they were simply afraid to disagree with Zhu Xi. The group that followed blindly and did inferior scholarship simply fell into a position of catering to their own preferences. Later generations of scholars emulated this and made it a habit.

23

The Song scholars frequently adhered to what they heard and inclined toward what they liked. They did not take the orthodox teachings of Confucius and Mencius as their basis. Rather, they established their own school of thought freely and they became caught in rigid doctrines. This deepened into a veiled obstinacy. Because of this, their teachings are frequently at variance with those of Confucius and Mencius.

If scholars don't insist on their own teachings and if they think with an open mind, they will probably realize my words aren't intended to be boastful, reckless remarks. However, those who adhere to dogmatic teachings of biased people become completely fixated. If we do not wash away old opinions and arrive at new ones,[74] we will not change bad habits, and it is certain that we will lapse into confusion throughout our lives.

On Learning from What Is Close at Hand

24

The Way of the true person is inherently easy and simple. Since it is easy, it is readily understood, and since it is so simple, it can be readily followed.[75] It is easy to know because it isn't difficult or incomprehensible. When it is easy to follow, it is practiced naturally and it is effective.[76] Because of these characteristics, there are many people who follow it. In *Mencius* it says, "The Way is like a wide road. It is not at all difficult to find. The trouble with people is simply that they do not look for it."[77] Similarly, in *Mencius* it says, "One who walks slowly, keeping behind his elders, is considered a well-mannered younger brother. . . . Walking slowly is surely not beyond the ability of any man. It is simply a matter of his not making the effort."[78]

In my opinion, the teaching of Confucius and Mencius offers a method to begin learning from what is close at hand. Being intrinsically simple, it is easy to know and to follow. Attaining a high level of learning is merely a natural result of beginning with what is close at hand. This is different from the learning of the Buddhists, who tend to relish abstractions and desire to enter the sphere of Nyorai Buddha all at once.[79] When Confucians of later ages established their teachings, they talked about things that were often abstract and lofty and thus especially difficult to fathom and to practice. In this they differed from the original teaching of Confucius and Mencius.

25

Confucius considered filiality, obedience, loyalty, and trustworthiness as fundamental, and he regarded learning as involving both study and practice. His approach is straightforward, like a great pathway. Even for foolish people it is easy to grasp and to practice. If we gradually make an earnest effort and investigate thoroughly the import of this approach, we will exert ourselves to the utmost and eventually master the details. This means we learn from things close at hand and progress to higher levels.

Song Confucian scholars, however, felt it was urgent to make it their first priority to pursue the truth by understanding the Supreme Ultimate [*taiji*] and the nonfinite [*wuji*], to pursue practice by quiet sitting and purifying the heart, and to pursue scholarship by detailed analysis. Being both lofty and abstract, and trivial and impractical, this learning of the Song Confucians came to be regarded as difficult to understand and to put into practice. Yet Song Confucian scholars took these useless and unimportant issues as their first priority.

This was different from the teachings established by the sages [e.g., Confucius and Mencius], who saw filiality, obedience, love, reverence, learning, practice, loyalty, and trust as primary. Those teachings established by the Song Confucians were too abstract and detailed, hence they were difficult to learn, to practice, and to embrace. People of later ages who studied those teachings were thus handicapped by the painstaking efforts to comprehend them and became bogged down.

26

Generally, we should consult with people who are intelligent, broadminded, and impartial on the doubts recorded here. We shouldn't argue with people who are obstinate, unintelligent, inferior scholars, or prejudiced. As it is said, "To speak with those who cannot be spoken to is to waste one's words."[80]

27

When we read ancient texts extensively, if we believe in them blindly, it is because we are misled. When we doubt indiscriminately because things are unclear, we become conceited. Believing what we think we should believe and doubting what we think we should doubt is the action of a wise person and is a superior way of learning. People who are intelligent do exactly this, but inferior scholars and foolish people cannot. In my opinion, since human beings are generally not sages, no one is without faults.[81] Even in the scholarship of former worthies, there are some points that do not correlate with

Confucius and Mencius, and their words are frequently contrary to the words of the sages. This is why we must choose carefully.

28

The *Analects* contains the teachings established by Confucius and his followers. It has set a standard for countless generations and has been a model throughout history. Nothing should be added to or subtracted from the text. The teachings of the later Song Confucians are excessive in their minute analysis and obscure in their arguments. In my opinion, their analysis is needlessly detailed. The more detailed it is, the more disjointed it becomes, and, because we are confused, clear understanding is impossible. Because of this, Song Confucian teachings became unintelligible and deviated from the teachings of Confucius.

The teachings of the sages are originally straightforward and easy, like a great road. They are not like a steep mountain path. When we analyze excessively, we meander down a confused and crooked path and we will not reach the great Way. This is because Song Confucian teachings differ from what Confucius taught.

The Indivisibility of the Nature of Heaven and Earth and One's Physical Nature

29

The teachings of the Song Confucians frequently differ from those of the sages [e.g., Confucius and Mencius]. In the *Classic of Changes* it says, "Yin and yang are the Way."[82] It defines the founding of the Way of Heaven as yin and yang.[83] We should know that when the movement of yin and yang is normal and undisturbed, it is the Way. When the movement is disordered, it is not the Way. Consequently, the sages never regarded principle and material force as two things.

But Zhu Xi did claim that principle and material force were definitely two things.[84] Confucius taught that, "by their nature, human beings closely resemble each other."[85] Zisi said, "We call human nature one's Heavenly destiny."[86] Similarly Mencius said, "Our body and complexion are given to us by Heaven,"[87] and, "Human nature is good."[88] These phrases refer to our original endowment that we all receive. Since we all receive it from Heaven, naturally there aren't two kinds of natures. Confucius, Zisi, and Mencius all had similar opinions.

Claiming that human nature is all the same refers to the goodness of human nature. Although there are differences of tall or short, fat or thin, wise or foolish in endowment, everyone receives a mind-and-heart that is capable of compassion, shame, modesty, and the discernment of right and wrong.[89] When human beings are born, each has his or her own Heavenly endowed, original nature, and in this respect we say, "Human nature is good." In the past and at present human nature is not so different and consequently we say that "human nature is the same."

All people, in the past and at present, have only one nature. It isn't necessary to divide the nature of Heaven and Earth and the physical nature. Is not the nature of Heaven and Earth embodied in one's physical nature? If one's physical nature is separate, how can one receive Heavenly nature? Isn't even one's physical nature derived from Heaven and Earth? Then one's physical nature is nothing but the nature of Heaven and Earth. We can't divide the two. Confucius and Mencius never spoke of two natures. The indivisibility of physical nature and Heaven and Earth is self-evident.

Human nature is the name of something that humans receive from Heaven. Dong Zhongshu said, "What we call human nature is the substance of life."[90] His definition of human nature is close to that of Confucius and Mencius. When we discuss the origin of human nature, it is uniformly good. This is the common root. When we speak of branches, the good begins to subdivide endlessly. How-

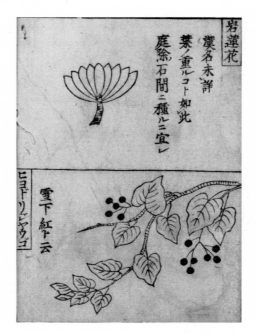

ever, it is probably a mistake to regard the nature of Yao and Shun as the same as that of ordinary people.[91] The reason is that Yao and Shun naturally have natures specifically for them, and ordinary people naturally have their own natures specifically for them. Since what each receives is different, we should not mistake it as one's own. The fact that the universe is not uniform reflects the actual state of affairs of the universe. This is the reason that many variations of human nature exist.

One's human nature is received at birth. The destiny one receives from Heaven is inherently good; it is without evil. It has a common origin. Indeed, individual human nature actually exists as an embodiment of the good that is one's Heavenly destiny. Yet when one originally receives material force, we would expect that there would be inconsistencies of purity and impurity, or thickness and thinness. After one receives material force, a person attains an individual, fixed nature. In this way, the human nature of wise or foolish people is not the same from the beginning.

In teaching others, the Song Confucians wanted to be very detailed. They regarded principle and material force as two. Moreover, in their doctrines they separated the nature of Heaven and Earth and physical nature. In doing this, they were excessively analytical. Confucius and Mencius spoke of human nature, but their explanations were clear without having to be analyzed. When Confucius said "similar," he meant that those of good nature are similar to each other. Therefore, the explanations of human nature by Confucius and Mencius should not be regarded as different. Even without detailed analysis their principles are clear.

A holistic approach is superior to minute analysis, for without [further] analysis the meaning is clear. If people who teach later generations follow the same line as Confucius and Mencius, they will be correct. If they establish different teachings because they follow lines different from Confucius and Mencius, that is unacceptable. The creation of things by Heaven and Earth begin and evolve gradually. This is the tendency of the movements of material force and the principle of nature.

Likewise, there are things that ancient peoples didn't discuss, and we must wait for them to emerge in later generations. It was often the case that Yao and Shun did not speak of something Confucius spoke of, that things which Confucius didn't speak of Mencius did, and that what Confucius and Mencius omitted, the Song Confucians addressed. The discussions of the Song Confucians are derived from the same source as Confucius and Mencius, and they clarify the explanations of Confucius and Mencius. That is why the Song Confucians contributed to spreading the Way of the sages. However, having granted this, there are some of their teachings that diverge from the words of Confucius and Mencius.

The Song Confucians explain the Supreme Ultimate by means of the nonfinite;[92] they regard principle and material force as two; they see yin and yang as not being the Way but as concrete things;[93] they think there is a nature of Heaven and Earth and a physical nature;[94] they explain innate goodness in terms of "human nature is principle."[95] This is not the same as the original intent of Confucius and Mencius, and the lineage of teachings is not the same. If scholars would examine this matter fairly, freed from flattery or bias toward the various Song teachers, they would perceive the differences.

Acknowledging Differences with the Song Confucians

30

In explaining the classics, it is permissible to have small differences in interpretation if they do not affect the Way. Since the Song Confucians' explanations of principle and material force, of the nonfinite, of the Way and concrete things, or of human nature and the Way, are all the foundation of moral principles, it is essential that there not be even small divergences from the words of the sages. If there are even slight differences in these areas, even though the concepts underlie the established doctrines of the earlier teachers, we should not accept them merely to indulge in flattery and servility. We should identify the differences by comparing them with the words of the sages. For when the doctrines are not correct, the Way does not become clear.

31

Zhu Xi said, "If people take an attitude that they don't rely on only one school and are not partial to only one theory, they will get a hodgepodge of knowledge even though they may be erudite."[96]

When I consider these words of Zhu Xi, I cannot help but doubt them. Why do I doubt them? If we can depend directly on the sages, as the seventy principal disciples of Confucius did,[97] it will be all right to have more than one school and more than one theory.

However, even though the Cheng brothers and Zhu Xi were highly intelligent men, when we think of devotion to the highest good, impartiality and lack of prejudice, I am afraid they were not the same as the sages. If people rely on only one explanation or incline toward one type of learning, inevitably they won't be able to comprehend with a broad perspective or open inquiry. Instead they will suffer from a wisdom obstructed by prejudiced and limited information. Prejudiced people, through flattery and servility, create factions and attack others for their personal gain. Such are my doubts, and I am unable to resolve them.

32

Later scholars should not have contempt for the worthies of the past and they should not thoughtlessly slander those who came before. Rather, they ought to show discretion. However, even the ancients weren't without some faults. In distinguishing between right and wrong, one shouldn't be swayed by undue deference.

33

Even if they are intelligent, those who come forward with their ideas may first offer ideas that are still not complete or detailed. A good example is that the ideas of the Cheng brothers and Zhu Xi differ somewhat from those of the sages. When later people discuss earlier people, even if they have only ordinary talents, they can still reflect on things from a different perspective. This is the advantage of those who come later in criticizing what came before. Thus, even criticisms by later people shouldn't be completely disregarded.

34

We later scholars[98] certainly cannot be compared with intelligent scholars of earlier times with regard to the loftiness and depth, or the greatness and smallness, or the breadth and narrowness of our learning. Naturally we should have a deep reverence toward the earlier Confucians.[99] However, later worthies also differ from the earlier sages[100] in impartiality and bias. Accordingly, even in the teachings of earlier Confucians, we should accept things that are in agreement with the words of the sages and we should believe what we think we should believe and doubt what we think we should doubt. In short, it is important to be selective.

35

From of old the changes in the spirit of the times continually move toward complexity and ostentation. This is the reason the present frivolous age has lost sight of what is essential. The condition of the world of past and present can't help but produce this result. Accordingly, in the ways of government and the arts of learning, we have an imperative duty to return to essentials and to avoid minute details. It is not necessary to emulate all the movements and transformations of the world.

Confucius was born in the declining period of the Zhou dynasty. Public opinion of that age regarded excessively cultivated people as gentlemen and simple people as rustics. Confucius wished to follow the ancients; he rejected ostentation and sought a return to simplicity. The age of Confucius was still close to an ancient, simple period, but a more worldly outlook had already developed by his day. Even more frivolous later ages lost simplicity and the spirit of the times degenerated daily toward excess. From the period of the Qin and the Han, times gradually changed and the world became increasingly complicated. Scholars living in today's world should place priority on simplicity but should gradually adapt to their age. If one rejects contemporary customs, there is no way to live in the world.

36

Song Confucian scholarship far surpassed that of the Han and the Tang in the explication of issues. However, the discussions of Song Confucians gradually became confused, their exegesis became more and more intricate, and their notes and explanations became extremely lengthy. In time the digressions became profuse and the arguments became increasingly detailed. In later ages this trend became a force like a flood, so that it was no longer possible to consider returning to the teachings of the sages. Because of that trend, simplicity declined daily. When later Confucians faced this way of scholarship, they were simply overwhelmed by the current pressing in from all sides. Even with strenuous effort they couldn't change embedded practices. Thus, they were not able to penetrate and reinvigorate ancient teachings and realize them personally.

Celebrated scholars appeared, but they only eagerly followed the current of the times. They couldn't change old customs and seek what was essential. Consequently, the path of later scholarship should be directed toward a change from minute details to essentials and from trivia to holistic integration by making people aware of this and changing old ways of scholarship. In my opinion there must be a suitable way for each age. Confucius followed the ancient sages, and scholars should do likewise. This is only my idea, but how do other scholars of today feel?

37

Are the Cheng brothers and Zhu Xi known as great scholars just because of the high level of their scholarship and insight? Even the greatness of their virtuous deeds is regarded as a model. The hetero-

dox scholars at the end of the Ming[101] attacked and despised the
Cheng brothers and Zhu Xi and, in addition, were contemptuous of
their deeds. While they pursued their studies, they didn't recognize
the profound knowledge of the earlier Confucians; they put on airs
and slandered them carelessly without respecting their virtue. This
is not the way of a true Confucian, but that of a petty person.[102] They
know neither others nor themselves. That is extremely foolish.

38

Zhu Xi, who was a superior person, aimed to transmit the sages'
teachings from the past and to open them up for future scholars.
For this reason his explanations and interpretations of the classics
were a blessing for later generations in their extremely detailed
analysis. These [interpretations] were sufficient without borrowing
troublesome explanations of later Confucians. They were also of
great benefit for subsequent generations.

Because Zhu Xi's explanations were very detailed, later Confucians just imitated such detail and analyzed things by blindly following the crowd. This resulted in confusion. Even though there are
numerous discussions by the later Confucians, they didn't add significantly to the great accomplishments of Zhu Xi. They were unable to develop his ideas further. What they added didn't contribute
anything, and when they did not add anything, there was no loss.
Furthermore, these people were unable to change old habits in their
scholarship. Thus, after the death of Zhu Xi, except for two or three
excellent people who made certain things clear, it would be fine if
many Confucians had kept silent.

39

Zhu Xi applied much of his energies toward the rejection of Buddhism. In my view, that was because formerly he had a very close
involvement with Buddhism and investigated the Buddhist way in-
tensely. It is understandable that his attacks penetrated deeply into

precise and subtle points. However, why in his ordinary discussions are there sometimes things that are similar to the heresies of Buddhism?

This coincidence probably derives from Zhou Dunyi's "Explanation of the Diagram of the Supreme Ultimate."[103] Zhu Xi's deep respect for Zhou Dunyi[104] was exactly the same reverence he showed to the sages. He accepted even a work that may not have been done by Zhou Dunyi. In my opinion, even assuming that Zhou did write this text, it reflected an earlier opinion that wasn't held throughout his life.[105] In Zhou's *Penetrating the Classic of Changes* there is no explanation concerning the nonfinite;[106] the contents of this text are not similar to "An Explanation of the Diagram of the Supreme Ultimate." Moreover, in the large collected works of the Cheng brothers, there is no mention of the nonfinite. This should be known.

40

The Confucian teachers of the Song were all intelligent men. Their scholarship and character far exceeded those of most people. The Confucians from the Han to the Tang didn't reach their level. However, their doctrines were somewhat close to the teachings of Buddhism and Daoism, and there are many dubious points. Most human beings aren't sages; they aren't without bias. To illustrate this, we realize that the light of the sun and the moon is not without shadows. Even a pearl shining like the moon is not without flaws. Shao Yong said: "Although Heaven gives birth to things, it cannot nourish them. Although the Earth can nourish things, it cannot create them. Although fire boils things, it cannot soak them. Although water soaks things, it cannot boil them. Even Heaven and Earth are not complete, and so why should fire and water be complete?"[107]

In my opinion, since Heaven and Earth are not perfect, how much more so is that true of wise men? How can they be without bias? Thus even though the scholarship of the Song Neo-Confucians is close to being pure and correct, it doesn't equal that of the sages. Hence, it is natural that it [betrays] occasional biases. We shouldn't rely on them completely and regard them as being wholly unbiased.

Surely the Way of the sages is fair and impartial. The sages hold fast to virtue so as to extend its influence widely.[108] In their actions they are skillful. Worthies who rank below the sages, although they are intelligent, probably do not possess virtue completely. The learning of the Song Confucians is genuine, but still it doesn't match that of the sages. They can't avoid having prejudicial personal viewpoints. Accordingly, frequently teachings have appeared that are different from the teachings of Confucius and Mencius. These include the following, which are the reasons for my own doubts: (1) taking the nonfinite as the basis of the Supreme Ultimate; (2) seeing principle and material force as two separate things; (3) dividing the nature of Heaven and Earth and human physical nature; (4) regarding yin and yang as not being the Way but as being concrete things below those that have form; (5) considering that which constitutes yin and yang to be the Way; (6) seeing material force and the physical body as having life and death; (7) regarding principle and nature as having no life and death; (8) regarding quiet sitting as a method of daily practice and regarding "holding to tranquility"[109] as a discipline for establishing the highest moral standard for human beings; (9) seeing the theories of Confucius and Mencius concerning nature as distinguished by their emphasis on physical nature and the nature of Heaven and Earth, respectively.[110]

41

Su Dongpo [Su Shi][111] remarked, "Even a superior person can't avoid being influenced by heterodoxy." I think the scholarship of Su was patently incorrect, and he himself, without knowing it, was affected by heterodox thinking.[112] However, his statement above has validity. Even if superior people hear the theories of followers of

Buddhism and Daoism, occasionally it is difficult for them to avoid becoming biased and obstinate by what they hear. These days obstinate and biased people think the learning of scholars of the Song is equal to that of Confucius and Mencius. They think the Song scholars have no weaknesses and that they are always right. However, I don't think that attitude is reasonable. The thinkers of the late Ming and early Qing harshly criticized the learning of various Song teachers as antithetical to the transmission of [the teachings of] Confucius and Mencius. They [the Ming and Qing teachers] were also followers of heretical teaching and extremely obstinate and biased. Their views are not reliable.

42

In the Ming period, Wang Yangming was an exceptionally gifted person. Many of his contemporaries were blindly enveloped by his scholarship as if they were swept away by a current that came rushing forth. In comparison with the Daoist "pure conversation" philosophers of the Jin,[113] Wang's scholarship did far greater harm.

Luo Qinshun[114] was a contemporary of Wang Yangming. He argued with Wang and criticized him. Luo should be regarded as a wise and superior person. In his learning, Luo Qinshun did not flatter the Song Confucians. He said, "Principle is only the principle of material force."[115] "Principle must be identified as an aspect of material force."[116] In my opinion, the Song Confucians improperly separated principle from material force, and later Confucians, flattering the Song Confucians, wouldn't question them. Only Luo, although he respected the Cheng brothers and Zhu Xi, did not flatter them, and his views were eminently sound. However, the various Confucian scholars of the later Song, Yuan, and Ming didn't say this. We ought to regard Luo as an outstanding scholar. Although both Xue Xuan[117] and Hu Juren[118] were first-rate Ming Confucians, their views were far inferior to those of Luo.

PART II

Partiality in the Learning of the Song Confucians

43

An ancient person said: "Frequently people do not realize that they are blinded by their own desires. There are indeed not a few people who are deluded by knowledge acquired from the senses."[119] In my humble opinion, from ancient times people have often been deluded [by sense knowledge]. Since the end of the Song, the number of prejudiced scholars who were deluded by sense knowledge and were not enlightened have been even more numerous. It is a problem on which scholars ought to reflect.

44

Following the end of the Song, Confucian scholarship was too focused on details, and, being verbose and rambling, it was confusing and overly intricate. Compared to the age of Confucius and Mencius, it is probably ten times or one hundred times more elaborate. The current [of elaborate scholarship] flows on, encompassing everything without limit, and we don't know where it will stop. Because there are scholars who cannot preserve what is brief and to the point, they have only wide knowledge without substantial results. To what is this due? Since the Song, scholarship has increased gradually in detail, disregarding the root and following the branches, being excessively analytical and incoherent. Isn't it because sound methods have been completely abandoned? Yet later Confucians continue to imitate those excesses. Consequently true virtue has disappeared.

45

Someone asked: "Can we rely completely on the words of the Cheng brothers and Zhu Xi? Moreover, is there any room to harbor doubts?" To this I answer that the words of the sages should, of course, be trusted for many generations. Next, the words of worthies should also be seen as models. However, words and deeds have a mutual relationship. If worthies are mistaken in their actions, one can also expect prejudice and partiality in their knowledge. It then follows that even in their theories and their scholarship, there are probably flaws such as bias and deficiencies of excess or omission. This fact is a natural dividing line between sages and worthies. When one's learning lacks prejudices and partiality, one approximates sagehood. From my point of view, the Cheng brothers and Zhu Xi are wise philosophers. Since Mencius, only a few people[120] can be regarded as knowing the Way. However, since we can't go so far as to say they are sages, their philosophy also is probably not equal to that of the sages. The theories of the Cheng brothers and Zhu Xi ought not to be taken lightly by later scholars. Even given that, we must have a discriminating attitude.

Mencius says, "If one believed everything in the *Book of History*, it would have been better for the book not to have existed at all. In the Wu cheng chapter I accept only two or three passages."[121] We should believe these words. The works of the Cheng brothers and Zhu Xi are very verbose, and, if we never doubt their words at all, we will come to accept these works completely. With regard to their theories, people nowadays bend and apologize; since they are primarily swayed by their own private opinions, they succumb to their own prejudices. They can't be regarded as impartial. I am a simple, ordinary person and am unable to be a loyal follower of the Cheng brothers and Zhu Xi. I do not indulge in flattery. On the other hand, as long as I don't indulge my own preferences, I am able to be faithful to the thinking of the Cheng brothers and Zhu Xi.

46

King Wu of the Zhou and his brother, the duke of Zhou,[122] were sages. Leading the way with the feudal lords and the princes, they subjugated the tyrant Zhou,[123] but I have never heard that people condemned that. Why did Boyi and Shuqi disapprove of King Wu?[124] This was because they could not comprehend the exercise of authority by the sage-king [in accordance with particular situations] even though they were praiseworthy for their independent views and unique conduct. However, their purity [of motivation] was indeed sagelike.[125] But their strong points revealed the partiality of their nature. Although they had great wisdom, they also had bias. The same thing can be said of the learning of several teachers of the Song. In the learning of the Song Confucians, the line of the Way is clear and correct, and, as their character and conduct were conscientious, they were among the genuine Confucians to have appeared since Mencius. But their theories are overly detailed and suffer from being too analytical. In this respect, they differ from the holistic theories of Confucius and Mencius. For example, at the end of the Zhou, external form overcame [internal] substance,[126] and this resulted in many scholars' promoting biased doctrines. The learning in the Song was increasingly biased, and there were many instances of teachings contrary to the sages.

Reverence Within and Rightness Without

47

Cheng Hao said, "In the learning of the Buddhists there is reverence to straighten the internal life but no rightness to square the external life."[127] I still can't understand these words. Buddhism has its own logic of substance and function. Buddhists take "emptiness and tranquility"[128] as substance and "no place to abide"[129] as function. Thus one cannot expect that the Buddhists' substance is using reverence to reform one's interior life. If the Buddhists have such a substance as reverence within, then they certainly have the function of correcting one's exterior by rightness. Then why must the Buddhists degenerate so much as to dispense with basic human relations? I cannot understand what Cheng Hao meant. The reason later Confucians tried in vain to explain this was simply because of their adulation of the Cheng brothers.

48

In the time of Yao and Shun, through the three ages of Xia, Shang, and Zhou, there were many among the lords and retainers who spoke of reverence, but there were few who spoke of loyalty and faithfulness. Why? The spirit of people of ancient times, being wholesome and cordial, was different from that of the decadent present period. As a result, the lords and retainers all had loyal natures. They didn't lose these traits even though they did not speak about loyalty or faithfulness as the first priority.[130] Reverence is a practice to be followed for the sake of making loyalty and faithfulness central. So if reverence is instilled within the heart, both loyalty and faithfulness will also emerge.

By the time of Confucius, we see that the world had gradually become decadent. Consequently, by taking loyalty and faithfulness as central, the Sage [Confucius] made these values the basis for culture and moral conduct.[131] By contrast, in more dissolute times, if scholars do not emphasize loyalty and faithfulness and rather emphasize reverence, they will definitely lack solid practices. Eventually there will be no one except those who are overly polite or ostentatious. These are the characteristics of small, hypocritical people and are not appropriate to the Way of the true person. Hereafter, scholars ought to make loyalty and faithfulness central. "Abiding in reverence" is simply a method of making loyalty and faithfulness central.

49

In recent times scholars of the Way[132] who were trying to establish a reputation by espousing Confucianism often neglected to consider loyalty and faithfulness as foundational. They promoted "abiding in reverence" to make a name for themselves. For them, to abide in reverence became a forced effort of restraint. People who had superficial gravity lost loyalty and faithfulness as central. They tried to preserve reverence by force, and this was not appropriate for a Way of abiding in reverence. On the contrary, they injured reverence.

50

The sages [e.g., Confucius and Mencius] give priority to filiality, obedience, loyalty, and faithfulness. Through this [priority] the foundation is established and the Way is born.[133] It is an approach that attends to practical things, beginning with things close at hand and ending with lofty and distant things. People who reach great heights start with what is close at hand; people who climb high mountains naturally begin from low places.[134] By following a sequence, one gradually progresses on the Way. Heterodox teachings, and present-day vulgar Confucianism, regard lofty and distant things as primary. They boast and wish to attain enlightenment in one leap. They are not able to make gradual progress by following a sequence. If we reflect deeply, we will see there is no logic in wishing to force progress. To do so is to neglect to pursue what is solid, and to follow what is empty [impractical].

Influences from Buddhism and Daoism

51

When Zhu Xi spoke, he frequently used Chan Buddhist expressions. In discussing the art of composition, he said, "Even after reading the classics, such as the *Record of the Historian*, the *History of the Former Han*, or the writings of Han Yu and Liu Zongyuan, if we are not enlightened we cut off the head of an old priest."[135] "If we hit someone, there is the trace of blood; if we strike someone, there is the clear mark of a stick."[136] Presumably because Zhu Xi was immersed in the study of Chan in his early years, he was not able to discard those teachings. This influence is also evident in his jokes. An example is a story about Huo Kuang's servant who came to life again.[137] The two Cheng brothers never mentioned these kinds of things.

52

"The Supreme Ultimate [*taiji*] and also the nonfinite [*wuji*]" are found in Dushun's *Huayan View of the Realm of the Dharmas*.[138] It was passed down from generation to generation and its influence extended even to Zhou Dunyi. The notions that "*taiji* originates from *wuji*" and that "abiding in reverence" establishes a fundamental mode for humans are concepts that have been derived from Buddhism and Daoism. Zhu Xi had the greatest respect for Zhou Dunyi, and, because he believed everything in Zhou's thought, he never doubted these ideas.[139]

53

The expression "Substance and function come from the same source and there is no gap between the manifest and the hidden"[140] is from the *Commentary on the Huayan Sutra*, by a Tang priest, Cheng Guan.[141] These two phrases are of Buddhist origin. Why did the Song Confucians regard Zhou Dunyi and the Cheng brothers as the first to teach this idea?

54

The flow of Confucian teachings is one lineage continuing through many ages. The Six Classics and the Four Books have myriad words and phrases, yet, having a common truth, they are consistent. Those who promulgate theories without following the sages, even if their words are those of superb scholars, may be doubted. If there are mistakes, they will only lead later scholars completely astray.

55

The way to read texts is to seek understanding by inquiring, by removing self-centered opinions, and by relying on the opinions of the sages and worthies. We should not add unneeded, useless words. If we follow these principles, eventually we will comprehend the true meaning of the sages. We should not forcefully promote our own egocentric opinions, nor should we be stubborn, contentious, or careless. If we tend in these directions even slightly, we won't be able to follow the thinking of the sages and worthies. Even earlier Confucians could not escape mistakes. If scholars have doubts with regard to earlier Confucians, they should not simply believe blindly. An ancient saying notes, "People think that whatever they learn is clearly correct." However, even superior people are not without failings. The Song Confucians believed in the Diagram of the Supreme Ultimate and in "An Explanation of the Diagram of the Supreme Ultimate," and they had biases. Having strong opinions and being zealous in learning, they revealed their biases. In perceiving a person's faults, we come to know their humaneness.[142]

56

Later scholars, of course, should show respect toward earlier Confucians. However, the path of learning is open to all.[143] When we make a judgment of right or wrong, we should base it on our own sound and impartial assessment. Why do scholars since the Song tend to make it a practice to flatter the earlier Confucians? How can their learning not be tainted?

57

Scholars who cling to prejudiced opinions, even though they have doubts regarding the Song Confucians, flatter them and conform to their ideas. Consequently, they spend their whole lives not realizing this. If there are people who harbor even slight doubts, they are frowned upon. They are regarded as biased and heretical, and they are consistently slandered. This is reprehensible and reflects a mistaken obstinacy.

58

The teaching of the sages is simple and direct; it doesn't have the defect of invoking strained or overly complicated interpretations. Later scholarship tends to be too fragmented; it doesn't have wholeness and balance. Thus, true scholars can't bear all the details. To like simplicity and to dislike detail is a common human feeling. The scholarship of later generations is fragmented; consequently, it is contrary to common human feeling. It is natural that ordinary people dislike that kind of scholarship. When the sages taught, they inspired students to make progress untiringly. When later Confucians taught, things were exactly the opposite.

59

When the petty person with few talents teaches, he has his self-assurance and he never doubts himself.[144] Not distinguishing between the truths and falsehoods of such persons, many people believe them and don't doubt them. Their teaching is not designed to inspire people with wisdom and virtue; it is merely a clever act.

60

If scholars do not follow the classics yet believe in latter-day biased opinions, then how can they realize their mistakes and examine the root of the Great Way?

A Discussion of the Metaphysical and the Physical

61

In the "Appended Judgments" of the *Classic of Changes* it says, "In Heaven configurations [patterns or shapes] are created; on Earth physical forms are created." It also says, "When something is manifested it is called configuration; what has taken physical form is called a concrete thing [material object]." Furthermore, it says, "What is above form is called the Way; what is below form is called a concrete thing."[145]

In my view, "physical form" means having concrete substance. "What is above" means in Heaven. "What is below" means on the Earth. What is "above form" is the material force [*qi*] of yin and yang; it is without shape and exists in Heaven. It is above the physical forms and the concrete objects of "the ten thousand things." That is why it is called "above form." "Configuration" means the refined aspects of forms, and they issue from above. The material force of yin and yang is above and its manifestation we call "becoming configurations." The two material forces (yin and yang) in Heaven operate and interact, and we call this the Way. What is called "physical forms below" refers to the concreteness of hardness and softness of all things that are in the Earth.[146] Physical forms are the concrete substances of shapes and they remain below. By possessing shape and substance, things are formed. We call them concrete objects.

Heaven exists above, Earth exists below.[147] Thus they are designated "upper" and "lower." The Way of Heaven is formless and has the configurations [patterns] of yin and yang. Thus it is said, "In Heaven patterns are formed." The Way of Earth, having physical forms, has concrete substance. As a result it is said, "In Earth physical forms are created." Hence in Heaven there are no physical forms, while on Earth there are physical forms. Doesn't the expression "In Heaven configurations are formed" refer to yin and yang? In Heaven yin and yang have neither form nor substance. However, the configurations are revealed due to the movement and transformation of the two material forces of yin and yang. Accordingly, "when something is manifest it is called configuration." In the *Classic of Changes* it says, "What establishes the Way of Heaven is called yin and yang."[148] This means in Heaven there are configurations that have no physical form or substance. Yin and yang flow, and this causes growth in all things.[149] This is the Way of Heaven.

The Way of Heaven is only yin and yang. There is nothing outside of yin and yang. Yin and yang alternate endlessly. We call this flow the Way. Doesn't the phrase "On Earth physical forms are cre-

ated" refer to the myriad things? The myriad things indicates mountains, rivers, the great Earth, human beings, and living things,
namely all that has shape and exists below. In the *Classic of Changes*
it says: "What establishes the Way of Earth is called hard and soft."[150]
This means that on the Earth there are shapes and they have the
characteristics of hardness or softness. These are called concrete
things.

The Cheng brothers explained that yin and yang also were below
form,[151] and Zhu Xi's *Original Meaning of the Classic of Changes* followed this interpretation.[152] There is constancy and transformation
in the operations of yin and yang. Constancy refers to what is genuine and correct in the operation; this is deemed the Way. Transformation refers to mishaps and biases in the operations; we cannot
regard it as the Way. The Cheng brothers and Zhu Xi considered yin
and yang to be below form, but that is dividing yin and yang and the
Way into two. They also separated principle and material force. They
explained it by contrasting the Way as principle with yin and yang as
concrete things. I have doubts about this because if we regard yin
and yang as below form and say, "In Heaven configurations are
formed," does this indicate only the sun and moon and the Heavenly bodies? If this is so, it is inconsistent with the explanation of
yin and yang as producing configurations. This is the first point of
disagreement.

That which is "below form" indicates that which has physical
shape and is on the Earth. Mountains, rivers, the great Earth, human beings, and living things are all concrete things. We call things
that have [physical] substance concrete things. Yin and yang have
no substance, so we can't call them concrete things. This is the second point of disagreement.

Yin and yang are in Heaven and form configurations. They do
not take shape on Earth. Yet the Cheng brothers and Zhu Xi say,
"Yin and yang are also below form." This is the third point of
disagreement.

カシドリ

クハツテウ
ツグミノ類也

淡菜
一名東海夫人

白貝
扁ク有横文味不美
殻白邑横條多シ其條
甚細也無雑邑純白也

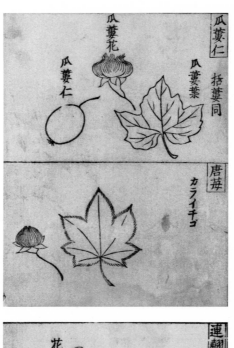

瓜蔞仁　栝蔞同

瓜蔞花

瓜蔞仁

瓜蔞葉

唐苺　カライチゴ

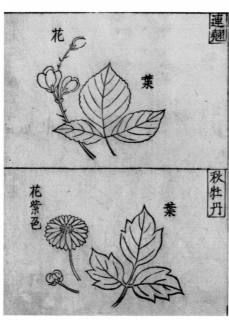

連翹

花

葉

秋牡丹

花紫色

葉

Again, in the *Classic of Changes* it says, "What establishes the Way of Heaven is called yin and yang." This indicates that the flow of the two material forces is the Way. Similarly, "What establishes the Way of Earth is called hard and soft." This indicates that concrete things are objects that take form through the characteristics of softness and hardness. This also doesn't regard yin and yang as being concrete things. This is the fourth point of disagreement.

As for the two characters of "above" and "below," they are clear when we say they refer to "existing in Heaven" and "existing on Earth." If it isn't so, the meaning of these two characters is difficult to understand. This is the fifth point of disagreement.

I still can't understand these explanations of the earlier [Song] Confucians. That is because they are different from the words of the Sage[153] in the *Classic of Changes*. However, I don't want to emphasize my own foolish opinion by criticizing earlier scholars. I am simply recording my doubts while awaiting the views of wiser individuals.

The Supreme Ultimate

62

In the "Appended Judgments" of the *Classic of Changes* it is stated: "In the changes there is the Supreme Ultimate [*taiji*] and it generates two forms."[154] Zhou Dunyi interpreted this as: "The nonfinite [*wuji*] and also the Supreme Ultimate [*taiji*]."[155] Zhu Xi said, "If we don't refer to the nonfinite, the Supreme Ultimate will be on the same level as things and thus we can't regard it as the origin of the transformation in all things."[156] In my view, the Supreme Ultimate is the name applicable to the material force in the state of chaos existing before yin and yang separated and the myriad things emerged. Nonetheless, it has the highest principle and so it is called the Supreme Ultimate. All the myriad things of Heaven and Earth are based on this. We don't speak of nothingness, we say "existence." In

other words, this implies that "in the changes the Supreme Ultimate exists." "*Wuji* and *taiji*" is an expression from Buddhism and
Daoism. Clearly it implies that "existence arises from nothingness."
In *Laozi* it says, "All things in the world come from being. And being comes from non-being."[157]

To regard nothingness as the origin and fundamental spirit of all
things is a Buddhist and Daoist idea. To regard existence as the origin and essence of all things is the teaching of the sages. Hence the
explanations concerning existence and nonexistence are the dividing line between the Way of the sages and other paths. We must
elucidate this carefully. If we wish to discuss the Supreme Ultimate,
we should not explain the character for nothingness as prior. The
Supreme Ultimate is formless; even a foolish person like myself
understands that. Therefore, on the question whether people would
misunderstand the Supreme Ultimate as a thing, we needn't worry
about it. Moreover, we should not regard the character for ultimate
to mean form.

In Zhu Xi's *Classified Conversations* he speaks of the nonfinite as
being without form,[158] but this does not express the original meaning of the phrase. Zhu Xi hoped that his discussions would be accepted without question and that people would have no doubts about
the veracity of "An Explanation of the Diagram of the Supreme Ultimate." Therefore, he overemphasized these words. Why were they
different from his ordinary, reasonable, and direct words?

63

In discussing Zhu Xi's remarks on "An Explanation of the Diagram
of the Supreme Ultimate," Lu Xiangshan commented that there is
certainly such a reality as the Supreme Ultimate. The sages clearly
indicated this. They did not establish their arguments with empty
words to mislead later generations with speeches and stories. "An

Explanation of the Diagram of the Supreme Ultimate" uses the term "nonfinite" at the beginning; but throughout Zhou Dunyi's book *Penetrating the Classic of Changes*, the term "nonfinite" is not used even once. The works of the Cheng brothers are quite numerous; however, they never used "nonfinite." Even if Zhou actually made the Diagram of the Supreme Ultimate in his early years, in his later years he never mentioned the nonfinite, and after he progressed in learning, it is clear that he no longer considered his earlier position correct.[159]

Lu Xiangshan also said: "In the changes, the Supreme Ultimate exists."[160] The sages spoke of the Supreme Ultimate; why do we now say "nonfinite"? When the Sage composed the "Appended Judgments,"[161] he did not mention the nonfinite. However, how could he have regarded the Supreme Ultimate as the same as a thing yet not as the basis of the myriad transformations?[162] He also observed: "Zhu Zifa[163] said 'Zhou Dunyi received the Diagram of the Supreme Ultimate from a Northern Song Daoist, Mu Bozhang, and it was transmitted to Mu by Chen Xiyi.'"[164] This had definitely been confirmed. The learning of Chen Xiyi is in the tradition of Laozi. The characters for nonfinite appear in *Laozi*.[165] The phrase is not in the classical texts of the Confucian sages.

In my view, if we look at these various statements of Lu with an open mind, they seem to be true. This one phrase of "the nonfinite and also the Supreme Ultimate" appears in the *Huayan View of the Realm of the Dharmas*, written by Dushun of the Tang.[166] It reflects a Buddhist theory, and we shouldn't call it Confucian. Despite his extensive learning, Zhu Xi didn't recognize this. The term "nonfinite" is originally Daoist. In a later period the Buddhists also adopted it because their way of thinking was similar. As Lu Xiangshan noted, the Diagram of the Supreme Ultimate first appeared with Chen Xiyi and it isn't found in the writings of the Confucian sages. These words are authoritative and naturally we should not deny their truth.

The phrase "the nonfinite and also the Supreme Ultimate" originally appeared in Buddhist texts.[167] Later, Zhou came to realize that
it had not been used by the sages. Thus, he did not mention nonfinite in his *Penetrating the Classic of Changes*, as Lu Xiangshan pointed
out. Since the nonfinite isn't mentioned in the collected works of
the Cheng brothers, we should realize that they didn't approve of
the theory of the nonfinite. *Laozi* says, "The nameless is the origin
of Heaven and Earth; the named is the mother of all things."[168] In
Laozi it is also stated, "All things in the world come from being. And
being comes from non-being."[169] The teaching of Laozi is that nonexistence precedes existence. The Confucian sages never spoke this
way. In other words, "the nonfinite and also the Supreme Ultimate"
implies Laozi's theory of the precedence of nonexistence over existence, and this means that existence arises from nothingness.

64

Chen Xiyi transmitted the Diagram of the Supreme Ultimate to Mu
Bozhang, and he in turn transmitted it to Zhou Dunyi. I think Chen
Xiyi and Mu Bozhang were followers of Daoist thought. Wang Zi-
quan[170] said, "Chen Xiyi studied under Shouya,[171] a priest of the
Helin temple." This probably explains the origin of the Diagram.

65

Zhu Xi's respect for Zhou was great. Thus, he did not suspect that
"An Explanation of the Diagram of the Supreme Ultimate" might be
an unfinished manuscript from Zhou's early years. He did not know
that its theory emerged from heterodox teachings and considered it
actually to be Zhou's composition. He revered it profoundly[172] and
devoted most of his efforts to it.

Fearing the doubts of various later Confucians, he defended it
vigorously and analyzed it in every aspect. Many of his arguments

and theories came out of it. Such an insightful scholar as Zhu Xi did this. How strange it is!

66

Hao Jingshan[173] said in *New Insights Acquired Through Constant Study*: "The learning of Zhou Dunyi was received from Chen Tuan[174] of Mount Hua." Someone added that Zhou, like Hu Wengong,[175] was taught by Shouya, a priest of the Helin temple of Runzhou.[176] There is now a small shrine for Zhou near the temple. Zhang Jingfu[177] said Zhou Dunyi was taught by Chen Tuan and he studied dwelling in tranquility. Consequently, for Zhou having purity and frankness of heart and being open-minded and without distractions were fundamental. For many Confucians the scholarship of the learning of the principles was influenced by Chan Buddhism.[178]

The Way and Concrete Things

67

In the "Appended Judgments" of the *Classic of Changes* it says, "What is above form is called the Way; what is below form is called a concrete thing." The material force of yin and yang is in Heaven and this is the Way. In other words, it is "above physical form." This force grows and alternates and becomes yin and yang. Material force is ceaselessly productive; being pure and without evil, it has principle and is not chaotic. Is this not the Way? When the primal material force of Heaven manifests itself on Earth, it evolves into physical form. This results in human beings and the myriad things. The evolution into physical form encompasses everything: mountains, rivers, grass, and trees; birds, animals, insects, and fish; frost, snow, rain, and dew. In other words, these are "what is below form." All physical forms on the Earth are referred to as concrete things.

68

Zhu Xi said, "Before Heaven and Earth existed there was principle."[179] He also said, "In the beginning there were no things. There was only principle."[180] It seems strange to me that these words are found in the learning of an enlightened, wise person. Zhu Xi's words are similar to those of Laozi, which assert that the Way creates Heaven and Earth and that existence arises from nonexistence.

Returning the World to Humaneness

69

"If for one day a person can subdue himself and return to propriety, all under Heaven [the world] will return to humaneness."[181] One day means for a sustained period. It refers to an ongoing period of moral practice. It does not mean it will be accomplished in one day. Disciplining oneself and returning to propriety is an extremely difficult thing. Sustained effort toward that must be made over a long period of time. How can one expect that it can be done in one day? The word "return" is the same as in *Mencius*, "The people return to humaneness."[182] It means returning and settling in a certain place. If one disciplines oneself and returns to propriety, the ill effects of selfish desires and the separation between oneself and one's environment disappear. Although the world is vast and people and things are numerous, the capacity of our heart extends to every place and forms one body with all things. If we abide within the circumference of a humane heart, love will be felt everywhere.

For example, it is like the human body. If one isn't sick and the circulation of *qi* and blood is good, *qi* flows throughout our entire body and becomes part of ourselves. This is returning to humaneness. If *qi* and blood circulate incompletely, the hands and feet will become numb and the skin will lose its sensitivity. Each part will seem no longer attached to oneself even though it is one's own body. In medical books this state of insensitivity is called a lack of humaneness.

Humaneness is regarding Heaven and Earth and all things as one body; it means that there is nothing that is alien to oneself.[183] Yang Shi thought that "humaneness was within everyone's own heart,"[184] and Lü Dalin also said "the expansive universe is within our own gate."[185] These are true statements. The saying "All under Heaven will return to humaneness" means if we are impartial, there is no room for selfish desires and love will be evident everywhere, even though the universe is so vast. This is also the meaning of the *Western Inscription*.[186]

Zhu Xi says, "If for one day we discipline ourselves and return to propriety, all people under Heaven will acknowledge their own humaneness."[187] This is to emphasize that the result will be very quick.

In my view the realization of humaneness can't occur in one day. The words of the sages are reliable and differ from the hyperbolic claims of the Buddhists and Daoists, who teach incoherent stories that lack common sense. In general, since there are actualities under Heaven, inevitably there are principles. If a person [a ruler] can discipline himself and return to humaneness just for one day, all people would praise him for his humaneness. But this is not attainable and, therefore, there is no such principle. Moreover, saying that there will be an immediate result in one day is boasting and contrasts markedly with the modest self-reflection of the sages.

Even though someone is praised by the world, it doesn't mean he must therefore be regarded as a humane person. Even a rebel like Wang Mang[188] was deceptive at first because he appeared to be a gentleman. People were deceived by him, and approximately 480,000 people praised his virtuous conduct in memorials to the throne. The ministers and leaders all said, "We should quickly increase his rewards." This is recorded in the *History of the Han Dynasty*.

From the above example, we can see that unless someone is truly humane, we should not call it humaneness even though the world praises it as humaneness. Conversely, if someone is truly humane, he does not lose humaneness even though there is no one who praises him. Although no one praised Tai Bo,[189] Confucius regarded him to be outstanding in virtue. Zhou Dunyi was very intelligent but only the Cheng brothers realized that;[190] other people did not appreciate it. However, there is no doubt that he was intelligent. The higher one's standards, the fewer the people who can meet them. However, many do not realize this and so a person can be [wrongly] regarded as benevolent. Just because many people praise a person, that does not mean such a person must be recognized as benevolent. Therefore, even if no one recognizes a person's humaneness, he could still be humane. The fact that everyone praises someone's humaneness is not sufficient reason to regard him as humane.

It says in the *Analects*, "How do you regard a person who is loved by all in his village?" Confucius replied, "We may not necessarily give our approval to him."[191] What we call the way of humaneness isn't derived from others' praise. That is why it is said: "The source of humaneness is in oneself; it cannot be gotten from others."[192] When the world praises humaneness, it is like the phrase: "To be famous if employed by the state; to be famous if employed by a ruling family."[193] To be praised by the whole world for humaneness is similar to "being famous." This is because both are derived from external appearances. They indicate reputation, not real achievement.[194] This perspective differs from what Confucius meant when he said, "Ah, who knows me; perhaps only Heaven."[195] Thus, the sage relied on himself rather than others.

It is more appropriate to interpret the character for "return" as meaning to "rest in" rather than "to praise." Kong Yingda of the Tang dynasty said, "The meaning of 'return' [in the *Analects*] is similar to its meaning in 'to return to the fundamental standard' of the

Great Plan in the *Book of Documents*."[196] Lü Zuqian said, "The character 'to return' in the returning to the fundamental standard is the same as the character 'to return' which means resting in one place."[197] These views are reliable and also tenable.

Hence, to say, "All under Heaven will return to humaneness" means that if one disciplines oneself and observes propriety, one's mind will be impartial and unselfish; one will see other people and other things as equal to oneself. All things under Heaven will be objects of love; they will all "return" and be part of one's humaneness. Humaneness is regarding Heaven and Earth and all things as being one body, inseparable from oneself.

However, even where Zhu Xi replies to Yang Shi,[198] the meaning is the same as in the *Commentary on the Analects*. Thus, Zhu Xi regards the saying "All under Heaven will return to humaneness" as an overstatement. It is also a lofty goal that one should not take lightly, yet I can't agree with this interpretation [by Zhu Xi]. On the contrary, I regard as true the explanation of Yang Shi and Lü Dalin, who say that all is complete within oneself. This viewpoint agrees with the original meaning of "all under Heaven will return to humaneness." We should not consider their statements as too lofty.[199] Although I disagree with Zhu's interpretation, I have merely recorded my opinion and I await the correction of wiser men in the future.

Reverence and Sincerity

70

Reverence is a method of preserving the heart that the sages transmitted through the ages. If one has reverence, one has virtue; if one does not have reverence, one does not have virtue. Therefore, the ancients believed that reverence was something that could protect[200] and foster virtue.[201] However, why did the sages regard loyalty and faithfulness as central, and why didn't they make reverence central?

Both sincerity and reverence are essential for the pursuit of learning. However, sincerity is the basis and reverence is the effort. It is fundamental to place priority on loyalty and faithfulness; such is the aim of learning. "Abiding in reverence" is a method for emphasizing loyalty and faithfulness; it cannot be the basis. The basis and the method are integrally related, but we must not confuse them. Sincerity and reverence are, of course, relative in their importance. It is like the relative importance of a ruler and his ministers; they cannot be equal. If we take reverence as central, reverence becomes primary and sincerity becomes secondary. Explaining the truth is like trying to balance scales—if one side is given too much weight, the other side will appear to have too little. When we overemphasize the centrality of reverence, surely loyalty and faithfulness are undervalued. If this occurs, although a person's outside appearance is solemn, within he may be frivolous. That means if sincerity is lacking, our actions will have no meaning.[202]

In regulating their conduct, scholars should necessarily combine ritual and music in order to attain a dignified seriousness and a peaceful composure. Why do they tend only toward a solemn seriousness? Obstinate people of today don't understand the meaning of reverence. They feel restrained by reverence and they become overly particular, stagnant, narrow-minded, rigid, and restricted. In their hearts they become withered and dried up, and they lack peace and joy. In relations with others, they have no compassion, warmth, or gentleness, and they are only severely critical of others. In their character, they lack humaneness and reciprocity. Their minds are restricted and tense and their appearance is not tranquil.

The Song Confucians greatly valued reverence[203] and regarded it as the master of the mind-and-heart. Scholars of later periods frequently imitated the worst of this tendency and valued only seriousness. They did not realize that loyalty, faithfulness, and compassion were most important. If we value only seriousness and severity, and if we undervalue loyalty, faithfulness, and compassion, we will become perversely solemn and cruel, and ultimately inhumane. Is this appropriate for a noble person?

71

The teaching of the sages was rooted in making loyalty and faithfulness central and making abiding in reverence the method. This is the teaching of the Confucian sages, which first builds up this root and next takes abiding in reverence as the method for making loyalty and faithfulness central. We must follow this sequence. The Song Confucians diligently made the virtue of reverence central. Since they weren't single-minded with regard to making loyalty and faithfulness central, their method was different from the method of the Confucian sages. Reverence is a method of self-cultivation; it is something appropriate for the sake of preserving sincerity. But the method of the sages makes loyalty and faithfulness central; I have not heard that it makes reverence central. If one tries to make loyalty and faithfulness central and also tries to make reverence central, then the mind will have two masters. Of course, we ought to respect the idea of abiding in reverence. However, we can't make it alone central.

Reverence as the Master of the Mind

72

Zhu Xi said, "Reverence is the master of [regulates] the mind-and-heart and is the basis of all things."[204] He believed that "disciplining oneself through reverence"[205] is the highest teaching of the sages. If one's mind-and-heart is not reverent, it will not be preserved. Thus he advocated reverence as a way to hold the moral mind firmly. This is the meaning of the statement "If we hold fast to the mind, the mind is preserved."[206] The expression "master" indicates a method for preserving the mind. This does not mean reverence is the master of the mind. The reader should not get caught in semantics and miss the real meaning.

Nonetheless, in the present period there are people who flatter Zhu Xi.[207] They say, "If we make reverence central to the mind, how can this harm the Way?" But I don't think these words are correct. Then what should we make the central basis of the human mind-and-heart? As Confucius says, "We should make loyalty and faithfulness central to the human mind-and-heart."[208] This is exactly what the *Doctrine of the Mean* says: "The attainment of sincerity is the Way of the human."[209] How could we abandon the Way of the human as central but adopt a method of clinging to reverence as central? No matter how virtuous and good the deeds can be, they cannot be regarded as central.

Reverence suffices as a method of self-discipline. Since [the time of] Yao and Shun, reverence has been a method of self-cultivation transmitted by the sages and worthies throughout history. However, since Confucius, Zengzi, Zisi, and Mencius didn't speak of regarding reverence as central, we should realize that it isn't consistent with the ancient sages and worthies to regard it as central.

Loyalty means one shouldn't be deceptive. This is substance. Faithfulness means one shouldn't be false. This is function. If we join loyalty and faithfulness, we have sincerity. Sincerity, being the master of the mind-and-heart, is the Way of humans.

In the *Classic of Changes* it says, "Loyalty and faithfulness are the methods of progressing toward virtue."[210] Without sincerity, even humaneness, duty, propriety, and wisdom are empty and artificial. If we don't make loyalty and faithfulness central, certainly the pursuit of learning will lack a foundation and we won't be able to progress. Reverence is, of course, a method that preserves the mind-and-heart. Reverence is something that fosters virtue. However, it cannot be regarded as the master of the mind-and-heart.

Sincerity is the true principle for humans;[211] it is having an authentic mind-and-heart. Accordingly, it is good to make a sincere mind-and-heart central, and we should not take the method of controlling the mind as central. The respect, intelligence, refinement, and reflection of Yao,[212] the gentle gravity of Shun,[213] the mindfulness of Yu,[214] the deep virtue of Tang, which progressed daily,[215] the cultivated virtue of Wen,[216] the conquest of laziness[217] of Tai Gong,[218] the straightening within and disciplining oneself through reverence of Confucius,[219] and the reverence described in the *Record of Rites*[220]— all are important methods of the sages for educating the people through self-discipline. The way of learning of the true person ought to value reverence. It is the method for making loyalty and faithfulness central. If there is reverence, we can attain sincerity. However, we can't regard reverence itself as the master of the mind-and-heart.

In the words of Cheng Mingdao, "Sincerity is the Way of Heaven; reverence is the root of human affairs. If we have reverence, we will become sincere."[221] I think it is good to call reverence the root of human affairs, but it is not good to call it central. As Confucius observed, "In Heaven there are not two suns, on Earth one shouldn't serve two rulers."[222] Similarly, how can there be two masters in the mind-and-heart of humans? If we regard loyalty and faithfulness as central and if we also regard reverence as central, it will be like having two masters in one mind. Among the virtues, we ought to distinguish between certain principal ones and other complementary ones. Loyalty and faithfulness are principal virtues, while the four virtues of humaneness, rightness, propriety, and wisdom are complementary virtues. If we make central what should be complementary, even though we may clearly be virtuous, we will be unable to avoid being flawed by vices.

If we incline too much toward humaneness, we are apt to be partial. If we incline toward duty, we are apt to be cruel. If we incline toward propriety, we are apt to be foolishly polite. If we incline toward wisdom, we are apt to be overly critical. How much more so if we make the method [of abiding in reverence] central? If a person makes reverence central and doesn't make loyalty and faithfulness central, he will tend to be outwardly solemn, overly careful about details, restrictive, fearful, and narrow-minded. The excesses are too numerous to count.

Those who stress reverence in the present day don't know the Way of reverence. Frequently they become externally solemn but in fact have a false austerity and formality. On the surface they appear self-disciplined and respectful, but actually they are arrogant and weak.[223] This is because they don't make loyalty and faithfulness central. Only those people who make loyalty and faithfulness central will be without fault. That is because making them central is the foundation of virtue. Loyalty and faithfulness are the sincerity of human beings and find their great source in the Way of Heaven.[224] The Way of human beings is the means by which the four virtues of humaneness, rightness, propriety, and wisdom are actualized. So, it is said, "Loyalty and faithfulness are the means to proceed toward virtue."[225] "These are the means by which the three virtues of wisdom, humaneness and courage are enacted."[226] We ought to call them regulators of the mind-and-heart.

73

The various Song teachers gave priority to the discussion of philosophy. Zhu Xi's *Reflections on Things at Hand*[227] places "An Explanation of the Diagram of the Supreme Ultimate" in the opening chapter. This makes the achievement of a "higher learning" primary and makes "basic learning" from what is close at hand secondary. This is different from the teachings of Confucius and Mencius.

74

The word "reverence" implies a method for disciplining the mind-and-heart that was transmitted from the ancient sages. We should clarify this by referring to the sages' explanations of reverence in the Six Classics and Four Books. The *Classic of Odes* notes, "Trembling with fear is like facing a deep abyss or walking on thin ice."[228] It also says, "We should be very careful."[229] The *Doctrine of the Mean* observes, "The superior person is cautious about what he does not see and apprehensive about what he does not hear."[230] In *Guanzi* it says, "What we think of as the mean [balance] is the foundation for one's words and deeds. From time immemorial, people who tried to accomplish something always began from here."[231] These are all explanations of reverence. The words are easy and the meaning is clear. Zhu Xi explained reverence in his later years and said, "Reverence is nothing but awe."[232] Sun Simiao is quoted in *Reflections on Things at Hand* as saying, "We want to be brave but cautious."[233]

In my view, awe is a correct explanation for reverence. Probably in explaining the word "reverence" we ought to rely first on these explanations. They are sufficient without being too wordy. It means, in short, holding fast to the mind and not letting go, and managing affairs with care. The explanations regarding reverence of the Song Confucians were recklessly profuse and extremely redundant. They overexerted themselves trying to explain reverence. In their studies they were too severe and tried too hard "to assist things."[234] Scholars became exhausted from rigid conventions and were inhibited by being overly careful or overly concerned about reverence. This was not like the teachings of the sages. I think that, since their attempts to preserve the mind were too intense and oppressive, their attitudes and external appearance were not relaxed and comfortable. Certainly one cannot maintain such a posture for a long time.

75

The Way that controls the mind is like the measuring of weights with scales. When we increase one side even a little, it becomes too heavy; when we decrease it even a little, it becomes too light. We only hope to have equilibrium. What I am getting at is that we should maintain a balance between "neglecting and forcing."[235] If we are overly careful, we probably cannot preserve reverence for a long time. In his leisure time at home Confucius was relaxed,[236] and so we should note that his daily life was calm and peaceful. Without this attitude even a wise person cannot preserve reverence for long, and the method of cultivating the mind-and-heart will suffer.

76

In *Correcting Youthful Ignorance* [Zhang Zai] says, "We are able to discuss human nature with those who know that death does not imply the end of a human being."[237] But in *Knowledge Painfully Acquired* [Luo Qinshun] says, "When there is this thing, there is this *li* (principle). Upon the disintegration of *qi*, there is death, and ultimately this thing returns to nothingness. When there is no longer this thing, there is no longer this *li*. How could there be this so-called death without annihilation?"[238] The Song Confucians [such as Zhang Zai] regard human nature as principle, and they seem to suggest that in material force there is no life and death; while in principle there is no life and death. This is a heterodox claim [to imply there is no death]. It is the same as saying, "One who dies but does not perish enjoys long life."[239] Using Luo Qinshun's explanation, we may counteract the errors of heterodox learning, and, moreover, we may dissolve the doubt of other scholars. In Zhang Zai's *Correcting Youthful Ignorance* there are also questionable points like this. The wisdom and learning of Zhang Zai was next only to that of the Cheng brothers. But his views are rough and incoherent and degenerate into heterodoxy. How frightening are the errors of learning!

77

Zhuangzi says, "With a little effort we can achieve significant results; this is the Way of the sages."[240] Although these words of

Zhuangzi are from heterodox learning [part of the Daoist tradition], we should believe them because the teaching of the ancient sages was originally concise and simple. The overly complicated scholarship and talkative discussions of the Song Confucians gradually became too intricate and incoherent. It is different from the Way of the sages, which is discussed in *Zhuangzi*.

78

The ancient sages regarded yin and yang as the Way and they didn't speak of the Way apart from yin and yang. The Song Confucians regarded the Way as separate from yin and yang and as something empty and void and without vitality or power.[241] They also regarded it as the root of all things and as the mystery of the Supreme Ultimate, but it was not the "Way of the sages." The Way of the sages is the life-giving principle found in Heaven and Earth. The original material force harmonizing yin and yang is ceaselessly fecund. Thus, in the *Doctrine of the Mean* it says, "The great Way of the sages is vast and causes the development and growth of all things."[242] It flows through the seasons and never stops. It is the root of all transformations and the place from which all things emerge. It is the origin of all that is received from Heaven and it is different from the emptiness that is taught in Buddhism and Daoism.

79

Principle is the principle of material force.[243] When a single material force flows through the four seasons, in origination, growth, gathering, and storing, there is no confusion; with a correct sequence, there is no disorder. Therefore, principle should be recognized in material force itself. For example, it is like water. The essence of water is its purity and tendency to flow downward. Water and what is pure and flows are, therefore, not two things. It is clear that we should not divide them and regard them as two. So, too, the material force of yin and yang, which is orderly and not chaotic, is the Way. If order and correctness are lacking, there is not the essence of material force. It is not the Way.

80

The teaching of the sages made propriety primary. The Song Confucians based their teachings mainly on principle. This was different from the teachings of the sages. The Song Confucians put lofty attainment before basic learning. For instance, they considered "An Explanation of the Diagram of the Supreme Ultimate" the first step in learning.[244] This also was different from the teachings of the sages. The words of the sage Confucius are regarded as an immutable model for learning. They are recorded in one volume of the *Analects*, and there is no need to look beyond this. If we do, we are likely to fall into heterodox learning.

The Inseparability of Principle and Material Force

81

When we begin to search for the wellspring of the Way of Heaven and Earth, it is not yet divided into yin and yang. Rather, there is a single primal undifferentiated material force. That is the state where highest principle exists but the configuration of yin and yang has not yet appeared. If we give it a name, it is called the "Supreme Ultimate" [*taiji*]. "Supreme" means highest and "Ultimate" means extreme. The Supreme Ultimate is the root of the Way and the origin of all things. Among all things, there is nothing more revered. We can't describe it sufficiently, so we refer to it as the Supreme Ultimate.[245]

The primal material force moves and alternates and it is called yang. That is the movement of the Supreme Ultimate. It moves and then becomes quiet. Being quiet, it congeals, and this is called yin. This is the tranquility of the Supreme Ultimate.

After it is tranquil, it moves and alternates between movement and tranquility, operating ceaselessly. Yin and yang are distinguished by the movement and tranquility of the primal material force. They are not two material forces. Yang is the movement of the one primal material force and yin is the congealing of the primal material force. Both are the activity and tranquility of the Supreme Ultimate. Confucius said, "In the changes there is the Supreme Ultimate and it gives rise to the yin and yang."[246]

If the single material force is not yet divided, the nebulous matter of the single primal material force may be regarded as the Supreme Ultimate.[247] When yin and yang are already divided, the Way of yin and yang is the movement of the Supreme Ultimate. The Supreme Ultimate and yin and yang are divided into before and after, and they have different names, but it is understood that there is no difference between them. The Supreme Ultimate is the revered name of the one primal material force before it divides into yin and yang. Yin and yang are the names of the Supreme Ultimate after dividing. In actuality it is not two things. Since yin and yang are divided through the movement and tranquility of the Supreme Ultimate, the flow of yin and yang may be called the principle of the Supreme Ultimate. In the *Classic of Changes* it says, "The alternation of yin and yang is the Way."[248]

The Way has the same connotation as a path; it is called this because it is a condition in which there is movement. That [condition] is the place of movement of the primal material force, and this is called the Way. Yin and yang are the movement and tranquility of the primal material force. Becoming yin and then yang, they alternate ceaselessly. In its primal undifferentiated condition, it is called the Supreme Ultimate; in the condition of flowing alternation, it is named the Way. Hence the Supreme Ultimate and the Way actually are one. The Way is the circulation of the Supreme Ultimate, and the Supreme Ultimate is the term used before the movement of the primal material force. The Way and the Supreme Ultimate are not two separate things.

The circulation of the two phases of yin and yang is logical, is not chaotic, is always orderly, and is called the Way. This is the essence of the two aspects of the primal material force. That which is confused and disorderly cannot be called the Way because it isn't natural.

Spring's warmth, summer's heat, autumn's cool, winter's cold are normal and correct and indicate Heaven's Way. If summer is cold and winter is warm, this is not normal and is not the Way. If yin and yang are normal, they are the Way. This is the original state of yin and yang and it is exactly the same as "establishing the Way of Heaven and calling it yin and yang."[249] Similarly, every year there is an unchanging order from growth to harvest. That too is the flow of yin and yang and is also called the Way. There is not something else in yin and yang that we call the Way. A Ming Confucian, Ke Shengqian, correctly observed that "the movement of material force is natural, and is called principle."

There is only one material force between Heaven and Earth, and when there is movement and tranquility, we call it yin and yang. The virtue of ceaseless production we call life [creativity]. In the *Classic of Changes* it says, "The great virtue of Heaven and Earth is called life."[250] The flow of this material force sometimes becomes yin and sometimes yang and we call it the Way. Since it has its logical and orderly flow, we also call it principle. Although the referents are not the same, and the names are different, it is actually all one reality.

Because of this, the movement of yin and yang is pure and orderly and this is the Way. Thus, principle and material force are definitely one, not two things. In other words, principle doesn't exist without material force and vice versa. Principle is not divided into before and after. No distinction can be made regarding temporal

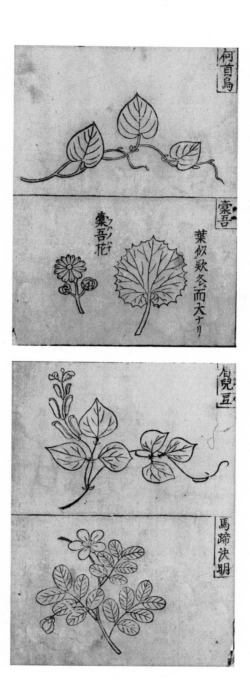

何首烏

囊吾

囊吾花

葉似欵冬而大ナリ

有兒豆

馬蹄決明

sequence. If there were no material force, how could principle exist? This is the reason principle and material force can't be separated. We can't say principle exists before and material force exists after,[251] and so we can't have a relationship of before and after. Again, principle and material force aren't two; we can't separate them. Principle is not something that exists separately; it is simply the principle of material force.

We call the Way the pure, orderly movement of material force. Since the movement is orderly and logical, it is called principle. The Way and principle are actually one thing. If we think that principle is one thing and resides only temporarily in material force, how is that different from the words of Laozi: "There was something undifferentiated and yet complete, which existed before Heaven and Earth,"[252] or the words of the Buddhists: "Something existed before Heaven and Earth and is shapeless. It is always the sovereign of the myriad forms, and following the four seasons it doesn't decay."[253] The material force of the great harmony of Heaven and Earth is the regularity of yin and yang. Because of this, it can create all things and becomes the basis of all things. This highest principle should not be scorned as a concrete object below form. Rather, principle and material force are one.

As movement and change are the Way's functions, it is ceaselessly producing and is called material force. As planting, growth, harvest, and storage follow a definite order without confusion, we call it principle. In reality these [principle and material force] are only one thing. However, when we call it principle, this refers to the purity and perfect goodness of material force. Thus, it can be described as unchanging. When we speak of material force as disorderly, this refers to those chaotic and turbulent aspects that lack regularity. This happens because material force moves, changes, and never stops. It then lacks regularity. However, this [chaotic stage] is not the original state of yin and yang. If we speak of the constancy of material force, we mean it is not disorderly. That constancy is the original state of material force. This is simply principle.

If we speak of water, we know water is originally pure. However, if it is mixed with mud, it loses purity and becomes dirty and polluted, but that dirtiness isn't the original state of the water. Material force has power that creates all things; therefore one may say that principle also has power that creates all things.[254] Yet if we say that principle has the power to create material force, it is wrong.[255] That is because "principle is the principle of material force." No distinction can be made regarding whether principle is prior or after material force, or whether principle is the foundation and material force is secondary. In a reply of Zhu Xi to Liu Shuwen,[256] he says that "principle and material force are definitely two things." His other views on this topic had the same implications. "The operations of yin and yang are the Way" is an explanation of the sages. These two positions are contradictory. I am at a loss and still unable to resolve them. I don't know which to choose.

NOTES

1. "Earlier Confucian" refers to Lu Xiangshan (1139–1193), a Neo-Confucian of the Southern Song period.

2. *Lu Xiangshan quanshu* [*Complete Works of Lu Xiangshan*], Sibu beiyao (Shanghai: Zhonghua shuji, 1927–1935), 35:29b (hereafter cited as SBBY).

3. *Zhuzi yulei* [*Classified Conversations of Zhu Xi*], ed. Li Jingde (Kyoto: Chūbun shuppansha, 1982), chap. 11, 296.

4. Zhu Xi said: "If our doubt is great our progress will be great. If we are aware of our progress and say that we have attained it, it proves that our progress has not yet been great" (ibid., chap. 115, 4414).

5. "Explanation of the Words and Sentences," in *Book of Changes*, trans. James Legge (New York: Dover, 1963), 416. "The Doctrine of the Mean" says: "When there is anything not yet studied, or studied but not yet understood, do not give up. When there is any question not yet asked, or asked but its answer is not yet known, do not give up" (*A Source Book in Chinese Philosophy,*

trans. and comp. Wing-tsit Chan [Princeton: Princeton University Press, 1963], 107).

6. *Analects* 2:4: "The Master said, 'At fifteen I set my heart on learning.'"

7. Yao and Shun are the two legendary sage-rulers of ancient China, with whom the *Classic of Documents* opens.

8. "The Counsels of the Great Yu," in *The Shu King*, vol. 3 of *The Chinese Classics*, trans. James Legge (Hong Kong: Hong Kong University Press, 1960), 61–62. This remark first appears as part of Yu's advice to Shun upon the latter's ascension to the throne. Orthodox Neo-Confucian interpretations of this remark, however, view it as "a message of the mind" passed from Yao to Shun, and then from Shun to Yu in conducting the coronation rites. For a discussion of this remark's importance in the Chinese intellectual tradition, see Wm. Theodore de Bary, *Neo-Confucian Orthodoxy and the Learning of the Mind-and-Heart* (New York: Columbia University Press, 1981), and *The Message in the Mind in Neo-Confucianism* (New York: Columbia University Press, 1988).

9. The five constant virtues are humaneness, wisdom, rightness, ritual decorum, and trustworthiness. See Zhu Xi, "The *Mean by Chapter and Phrase*," and Xu Heng, "Straight Talk on the Essentials of the *Great Learning*," in *Sources of Chinese Tradition*, ed. Wm. Theodore de Bary and Irene Bloom (New York: Columbia University Press, 1999), 1:735, 771.

10. These are often referred to as the "three dynasties" of ancient China, dating from approximately the second millennium to the third century B.C.E.

11. Han dynasty (202 B.C.E.–220 C.E.); Tang dynasty (618–906).

12. Song dynasty (960–1279). The teachers referred to here are presumably Zhou Dunyi (1017–1073), Shao Yong (1011–1077), Zhang Zai (1020–1077), Cheng Hao (1032–1085), Cheng Yi (1033–1107), and Zhu Xi (1130–1200).

13. Pi Yong, *Zhongguo zixue mingzhu jizheng* [*Commentaries on the Comprehensive Discussions in the White Tiger Hall*], Baihu tong shuzheng, 86: 302–303.

14. *Zhuzi yulei*, chap. 115, 4414.

15. Zhou Dunyi, "Explanation of the Diagram of the Supreme Polarity" (*Taiji tushuo*), in *Sources of Chinese Tradition*, ed. de Bary and Bloom, 1:673. See also Zhu Xi, *Reflections on Things at Hand*, trans. Wing-tsit Chan (New York: Columbia University Press, 1967), 5: "The Ultimate of Nonbeing [*wuji*] and also the Supreme Ultimate [*taiji*]."

16. Zhu Xi said: "Fundamentally principle and material force cannot be spoken of as prior or posterior. But if we must trace their origin, we are

obliged to say that principle is prior. However, principle is not a separate entity. It exists right in material force" ("Principle [*Li*] and Material Force [*Ch'i*]," in *Source Book*, trans. Chan, 634).

17. Chen Beixi, *Neo-Confucian Terms Explained: The Pei-hsi tzu-i*, trans. Wing-tsit Chan (New York: Columbia University Press, 1986), 110. The *Classic of Changes* states, "'The successive movement of yin and yang constitutes the Way.' Yin and yang are material forces and are below physical form. The Way is principle. It is simply the principle of yin and yang and is above physical form."

18. Chen Beixi said: "Physical nature is spoken of in terms of endowment with material force, while the nature of Heaven and Earth is spoken of in terms of the great foundation [principle]. In reality, the nature of Heaven and Earth is not separated from physical nature. The idea is to distinguish the nature of Heaven and Earth from physical nature" (*Neo-Confucian Terms Explained*, 54).

19. Zhu Zhi said: "The nature of man and things is nothing but principle and cannot be spoken of in terms of integration and disintegration. That which integrates to produce life and disintegrates to produce death is only material force. . . . As to principle, fundamentally it does not exist or cease to exist because of such integration or disintegration" ("Principle [*Li*] and Material Force [*Ch'i*]," in *Source Book*, trans. Chan, 637–638).

20. Zhou Dunyi said: "'The state of absolute quiet and inactivity' is sincerity. . . . Sincerity is infinitely pure and hence evident. . . . The sage is one who is in the state of sincerity" ("Sagehood," in *Tongshu* [*Penetrating the Classic of Changes*], in *Source Book*, trans. Chan, 467). He also said: "The sage settles these affairs by the principles of the Mean, correctness, humanity, and rightness (for the way of the sage is none other than these four), regarding tranquility as fundamental. (Having no desire, there will therefore be tranquility)" ("An Explanation of the Diagram of the Great Ultimate," in ibid., 463).

21. Li Yanping, *Yanping dawen* [*Dialogues with Yanping*], ed. Okada Takehiko, Kinsei kanseki sōkan, shisōhen, 8:9–13, 64–65, 114. Quiet sitting was a practice of self-cultivation taught to Zhu Xi by Li Yanping, a student of the Cheng brothers.

22. "Treatise on the Symbols," in *Book of Changes*, trans. Legge, 256; *The I Ching, or Book of Changes*, trans. Richard Wilhelm and, from the German, Cary F. Baynes, Bollingen Series 19 (Princeton: Princeton University Press, 1967), 653; *A Concordance to Yi ching*, Harvard-Yenching Institute Sinological Index Series, supplement no. 10 (Taibei: Chinese Materials and Research

Aids Service Center, 1973), 32: "When one's movements and restings all take place at the proper time for them, one's way of proceeding is brilliant and intelligent."

23. Chen Beixi said: "The mind is the master of the body because it possesses an unobstructed intelligent consciousness" (*Neo-Confucian Terms Explained*, 56).

24. Cheng Yi, *Yi shu* [*Surviving Works of Yiquan*], in *Er Cheng quanshu* [*Complete Works of the Cheng Brothers*] (Kyoto: Chūbun shuppansha, 1979), chap. 16, 455.

25. Qin dynasty (221–207 B.C.E.).

26. For a discussion of Zhu Xi's views on the *Classic of Changes*, see Zhang Liwen, "An Analysis of Zhu Xi's System of Thought of I," in *Chu Hsi and Neo-Confucianism*, ed. Wing-tsit Chan (Honolulu: University of Hawaii Press, 1986), 292–311.

27. Lu Yu (*hao*, Fangweng; *zi*, Wuguan; 1125–1210) was a poet of the Song dynasty. For a brief account of his life, see D. R. Jonker, "Lu Yu," in *Sung Biographies*, ed. Herbert Franke (Wiesbaden: Steiner, 1976), 2:691–704. For the quote, see Lu Yu, *Weinan wenji*, 29.

28. "He who tries to be sincere is one who chooses the good and holds fast to it" ("Doctrine of the Mean," in *Source Book*, trans. Chan, 107).

29. "The Way of learning to be great (or adult education) consists in manifesting the clear character, loving the people, and abiding in the highest good" ("The Great Learning," in ibid., 86).

30. "Confucius said, 'Shun was indeed a man of great wisdom! He loved to question others and to examine their words, however ordinary. . . . This was how he became Shun (the sage-emperor)'" ("Doctrine of the Mean," in ibid., 99).

31. "Shuoshan xun" [Explaining Mountains], in *Huainanzi* [*The Art of Rulership*], Kokuyaku kanbun taisei, keishi shibu (Tokyo: Tōyō bunka kyōkai, 1955), 11:419.

32. "Biography of Liu Liang," in *Hou Han shu* [*History of the Later Han Dynasty*] (Beijing: Zhonghua shuju, 1966), chap. 80B, 2635.

33. *Analects* 15:39.

34. "The Great Appendix," in *Book of Changes*, trans. Legge, 389.

35. The Six Classics are the *Classic of Changes* (*Yijing*), *Classic of Documents* (*Shujing*), *Classic of Odes* (*Shijing*), *Spring and Autumn Annals* (*Chunqiu*), *Record of Rites* (*Liji*), and *Record of Music* (*Yueji* [not extant]).

36. "Great Appendix," in *Book of Changes*, trans. Legge, 355.

37. Cheng Yi interpreted the phrase in the *Classic of Changes* as follows:

"The Way is not the same as yin and yang but that by which yin and yang succeed each other. It is like Change, which is the succession of closing (contracting) and opening (expanding)" ("Selected Sayings," in *Source Book*, trans. Chan, 552). Zhu Xi also adopted this interpretation, which led to the view of material force as separate from principle. Principle, which is inherent in yin and yang, is one, and material objects produced by them are the other. Ekken opposed this interpretation; he regarded material force and principle as one entity.

38. Zhu Xi equivocated on this issue. While he sometimes stated that "principle is not a separate entity. It exists right in material force" ("Principle [*Li*] and Material Force [*Ch'i*]," in *Source Book*, trans. Chan, 634), he also remarked, "What are called principle and material force are certainly two different entities" (637). Ekken disagreed with the latter claim.

39. According to Zhu Xi, "Fundamentally principle and material force cannot be spoken of as prior or posterior. But if we must trace their origin, we are obliged to say that principle is prior" (ibid., 634). Here, Zhu Xi equivocated, stating that on the one hand, principle and material force cannot be spoken of in terms of priority or posteriority. However, Ekken disagreed with his final statement that principle is prior.

40. "In antiquity the sages wrote the *Book of Changes*, . . . in founding the way of heaven, they spoke of yin and yang" ("Discourse on the Trigrams," in *Book of Changes*, trans. Legge, 423).

41. Zhu Xi said: "The nature of human beings and things is nothing but principle and cannot be spoken of in terms of integration and disintegration. That which integrates to produce life and disintegrates to produce death is only material force and what we call the spirit, the soul and consciousness are all effects of material force" ("Principle and Material-Force," in *Sources of Chinese Tradition*, ed. de Bary and Bloom, 1:701).

42. Yi T'oegye (1501–1570), an orthodox Neo-Confucian scholar in Korea whose ideas strongly influenced thinkers in the Yi dynasty, compiled *Record of Self-Reflections*, a collection of letters written to his students. See *T'oegye chonso* [*The Complete Works of Yi Hwang*], 5 vols. (Seoul: Songgyun'gwan University Press, 1986).

43. *Analects* 1:14: "A gentleman associates with those who possess the Way and thereby corrects his faults."

44. Ekken's view differs from that of Zhu Xi, who says principle is not destroyed ("Principle and Material-Force," in *Sources of Chinese Tradition*, ed. de Bary and Bloom, 1:701).

45. Cheng I (Cheng Yi), "Selected Sayings," in *Source Book*, trans. Chan,

569. Zhu Xi also supported the view that "human nature is principle" (*Reflections on Things at Hand*, 28–29). Zhu distinguished the original mind as good. When it is aroused and expresses itself in feelings, good and evil arise. One's original nature is based on principle and is always good. However, one's capacity is based on *qi*, which is not always clear. Thus capacity may be good or evil.

46. "What Heaven (*Tian*, Nature) imparts to man is called human nature" ("Doctrine of the Mean," in *Source Book*, trans. Chan, 98).

47. *Mencius* 7A:38. References here and subsequently are to *Mencius*, trans. D. C. Lau (Harmondsworth: Penguin, 1970).

48. Zisi (483–402? B.C.E.), a grandson of Confucius, is considered to be the author of the *Doctrine of the Mean*, as is suggested by the Guodian materials.

49. Jie, the last king of the Xia dynasty, indulged his wife at the expense of the people. He was subjugated by King Tang of the Shang.

50. The last king of the Shang dynasty, Zhu Zhou, lived a decadent life. Because of this, he could not win the people's support and was killed by King Wu of the Zhou. Zhou is regarded as a prototype of a tyrant.

51. Zi Yue was a man of the Spring and Autumn period. See *Zuozhuan zhushu* [*Commentaries on Zuozhuan*], SBBY, 21:11b.

52. This is in contrast to original nature, which is perfectly good. Physical nature may be directed toward evil when material force is received in its state of obscurity or obstruction.

53. Confucius made this distinction about human nature and practice: "By nature men are alike. Through practice they have become far apart" (*Analects* 17:2, in *Source Book*, trans. Chan, 45).

54. Emperor Yang (569–618), the son of Emperor Wen of the Sui dynasty, killed his father and tyrannized the people.

55. Luo Qinshun (1465–1547), a Neo-Confucian scholar of the Ming era, explains this theory in *Kunzhiji*. See *Knowledge Painfully Acquired: The K'un-chih chi by Lo Ch'in-shun*, trans. Irene Bloom (New York: Columbia University Press, 1987), 23.

56. *Mencius* 6B:2.

57. *Analects* 17:2. According to Confucius, the essence of human nature does not vary greatly; each person becomes different depending on acquired habits and customs.

58. *Analects* 17:3.

59. Boyi was an upright gentleman of the late Shang period. He attempted

to dissuade King Wu of the Zhou from executing the tyrant Zhou of the Shang, thinking it not permissible for a retainer to put his sovereign to death. However, his admonishments were rejected. He refused the offer of a stipend and went into hiding in the mountains, where he lived on brackens and eventually starved to death. See *Mencius* 2A:9 and *Records of the Historian: Chapters from the Shih Chi of Ssu-ma Ch'ien*, trans. Burton Watson (New York: Columbia University Press, 1969), 11–15.

60. Liuxia Hui was a wise man of the Spring and Autumn period. He was not ashamed of serving a prince with a bad reputation, nor did he disdain a modest post. See *Mencius* 2A:9.

61. Mencius said: "Boyi was too straight-laced; Liuxia Hui was not dignified enough" (ibid.).

62. This idea of opening up the sages' teaching for future scholars is essential to Ekken's own goals, which he sees as closer to those of Confucius than to those of some of the later Neo-Confucians.

63. "Recent times" refers to the Yuan, Ming, and early Qing periods.

64. "New learning" refers to Neo-Confucianism after the Song era.

65. "Classical learning" refers to Confucianism before the Song era.

66. In the later Ming period, many Confucians were under the influence of Wang Yangming's teaching, which emphasized innate knowledge, or "good knowing." Self-perfection consisted of remaining true to this innate sense of right and wrong. They thus rejected exhaustive investigation into the principles of things external to the mind, or the prolonged study of the classics.

67. *Analects* 17:24.

68. *Analects* 15:7.

69. Xu Weichang (171–218) was a poet of the Later Han.

70. Quoted in "Gui yan" [Valuing One's Words], in *Zhonglun* [*Discussion of Centrality*], Zhongguo zixuan mingzhu jicheng, 30:192.

71. *Conversations of the States* [*Guoyu*] (Shanghai: Shanghai guji chubanshe, 1978), 92. The work, whose authorship is ascribed to Zuo Qiuming (fifth century B.C.E.), is a history of the Spring and Autumn period in twenty-one volumes.

72. *Mencius* 7B:15.

73. *Mencius* 1A:7.

74. Zhang Zai said: "If one has doubt in the search for truth, wash away old opinions and arrive at new ones" (*Zhangzi quanshu* [*Complete Works of Zhang Zai*], SBBY, 7:3b).

75. "Great Appenix," in *Book of Changes*, trans. Legge, 349.

76. "If it is easy to follow, it obtains good results" (ibid.).

77. *Mencius* 6B:2.

78. Ibid.

79. A poem written by a Chan Buddhist priest, Xuanjue (d. 713), of the Tang says: "To enter the sphere of Nyorai Buddha [Enlightenment] with one step" (*Yongjia zhengdao ge* [Taipei: Foguang wenhua shiye youxian gongsi, 1997]).

80. *Analects* 15:7.

81. "No one is without faults. To correct one's faults is the greatest goodness" ("Xuan Gong," in *Chunqiu Zuozhuan jijie* [Shanghai: Shanghai guji chubanshe, 1978], 539).

82. "Great Appendix," in *Book of Changes*, trans. Legge, 355.

83. Ibid.

84. Zhu Xi said: "What are called principle and material force are certainly two different entities. But considered from the standpoint of things, the two entities are merged one with the other and cannot be separated with each in a different place. However, this does not destroy the fact that the two entities are each an entity in itself" ("Principle [*Li*] and Material Force [*Ch'i*]," in *Source Book*, trans. Chan, 637).

85. *Analects* 17:2.

86. "What Heaven (*Tian*, Nature) imparts to man is called human nature" ("Doctrine of the Mean," in *Source Book*, trans. Chan, 98).

87. *Mencius* 7A:38.

88. *Mencius* 6A:2.

89. *Mencius* 2A:6.

90. Dong Zhongshu (179–104 B.C.E.), a scholar of the Former Han, contributed greatly to the formulation of Han Confucianism. He believed the original nature of human beings had the potential for good but was not yet actually good. Humans would gain actual goodness under the transforming and civilizing influence of the rulers' teachings. See Dong Zhongshu, "An In-Depth Examination of Names and Designations," in *Sources of Chinese Tradition*, ed. de Bary and Bloom, 1:304, and, for his biography, *Han shu* [*History of the Former Han Dynasty*], SBBY, 56:4a.

91. In the opening paragraph of the *Commentary on Mencius* 3A:1, Zhu Xi says: "The nature of Yao and Shun is not different from that of ordinary people from the outset" (*Sishu zhangju jizhu*, 251).

92. The word *wuji* was first employed by Laozi and became popular through Zhou Dunyi's phrase "the *wuji* and also the *taiji*" in "An Explanation of the Diagram of the Supreme Ultimate" ("Explanation of the Diagram of

the Supreme Polarity," in *Sources of Chinese Tradition*, ed. de Bary and Bloom, 1:673). Zhu Xi accepted the concept of *wuji* and explained *taiji* by means of *wuji*, whereas Lu Xiangshan denied the idea of *wuji*. Ekken supported Lu's position, although he also had respect for Zhu Xi's philosophy.

93. In the *Explanation on Penetrating the Classic of Changes*, Zhu Xi wrote: "Yin and yang are material forces. They are the concrete things below form. The basis for yin and yang is principle. It is above form. The Way is the principle" (*Zhou Dunyi ji [Collected Writings of Zhou Dunyi]* [Beijing: Zhonghua shuju, 1990], 13).

94. The nature of Heaven and Earth is also called an original nature or a heavenly destined nature. This is based on a passage from Zhang Zai, *Zhengmeng (Correcting Youthful Ignorance)*: "After form is taken, a physical nature comes into being. When it is successfully changed, there exists a nature of Heaven and Earth" (*Zhang Zai ji* [Beijing: Zhonghua shuju, 1978], 23; "Enlightenment Resulting from Sincerity," in *Source Book*, trans. Chan, 511). "With the existence of physical form, there exists physical nature. If one skillfully returns to the original nature endowed by Heaven and Earth, then it will be preserved." Zhu Xi claimed there is a nature of Heaven and Earth and a physical nature. Ekken was, on the other hand, against distinguishing a physical nature from the nature of Heaven and Earth.

95. Zhu Xi, *Reflections on Things at Hand*, 28.

96. *Zhuzi wenji [Collection of Literary Works of Zhu Xi]*, Kinsei kanseki sōkan, shisōhen, 14:2914.

97. It is said there were three thousand disciples of Confucius, of whom only seventy were principal.

98. "Later scholars" refers to Ekken's contemporaries.

99. Ekken seems to be referring to the Song Confucians, especially the Cheng brothers and Zhu Xi.

100. "Earlier sages" refers to Confucius and Mencius.

101. "Heterodox scholars . . . Ming" refers to followers of the Wang Yangming school.

102. *Analects* 6:13: "You should be a true scholar. You must not be a petty scholar."

103. In "An Explanation of the Diagram of the Great Ultimate," Zhou characterized the Supreme Ultimate as nonfinite (*Source Book*, trans. Chan, 463–465).

104. Zhu Xi wrote that "Zhou Dunyi got to know the secret which had not been transmitted since the age of the sages" (*Zhuzi wenji*, SBBY, 36:9a).

105. Lu Xiangshan said: "When Zhou Dunyi wrote *Penetrating the Classic of Changes*, he did not talk about *wuji*. In my opinion, this is because he already knew the idea of *wuji* was wrong" (*Lu Jiuyuan ji* [*Collected Works of Lu Xiangshan*] [Beijing: Zhonghua shuju, 1980], 22–23). Lu is quoting the view of his brother, Lu Jiushao.

106. Chou Tun-i (Zhou Dunyi), "Penetrating the Book of Changes," in *Source Book*, trans. Chan, 465–480.

107. Shao Yong, "Zhi luan yin," in *Yi quan ji rangji* [*Collected Poems of Shao Yong*], 16:6b, in *Siku quanshu* (Taipei: Shangwu yinshuguan, 1983–1986). Shao Yong (960–1127) was a Confucian of the Northern Song period.

108. Zizhang wrote: "He who sides with moral force but only to a limited extent, who believes in the Way, but without conviction, how can one count him as with us, how can one count him as not with us?" (*Analects* 19:2).

109. In "An Explanation of the Diagram of the Great Ultimate," Zhou Dunyi stated that by holding to tranquility one establishes the highest moral model for the human. One is required to have no selfish desires in order to be tranquil (*Source Book*, trans. Chan, 463).

110. The Song Confucians believed that when Confucius said, "By nature close together; by practice set apart" (*Analects* 17:2), he was referring to physical nature, whereas Mencius was referring to the nature of Heaven and Earth when he said, "Human nature is good" (*Mencius* 6A:2).

111. Su Shi (1036–1101) was a literatus of the Northern Song period.

112. Su Shi's thought reflected the influence of Buddhism and Daoism and was quite liberal. Because of these characteristics scholars of the Cheng-Zhu school regarded him as heterodox.

113. From the period of the Three Kingdoms to the Jin dynasty, the Daoist transcendentalist philosophy became very popular. The Confucians felt that during this time people loved to discuss lofty subjects and thus ignored decorum and moral thinking. That trend resulted in social disorder and so was condemned. This kind of sophist thinking was labeled *qingtan* and disparaged as rhetoric over substance.

114. Luo Qinshun, the author of *Kunzhiji* (*Knowledge Painfully Acquired*), questioned Wang's theory about the innate knowledge of the good and Zhu Xi's ideas on principle and material force.

115. Luo, *Knowledge Painfully Acquired*, 173.

116. Ibid., 134.

117. Xue Xuan (1389–1464), a Ming scholar of Zhu Xi, emphasized self-cultivation and practice. He wrote *Record of My Reading* (twenty-three volumes).

118. Hu Juren (1434–1484) was a Ming scholar of Zhu Xi who served as a director of the Academy of the White Deer Hollow. He emphasized abiding in reverence and observed the orthodoxy of the Cheng-Zhu school, although he revised Zhu's ideas on principle and material force. He is the author of *Record of Occupying One's Sphere of Activity* (eight volumes).

119. Source unknown.

120. "A few people" refers to the Cheng brothers and Zhu Xi.

121. *Mencius* 7B:3.

122. King Wu and his brother, the duke of Zhou, were sons of King Wen.

123. The *Classic of Documents* records that "the tyrant Zhou wielded his power excessively" (*Shu King*, trans. Legge, 296). In *Mencius* 1B:8, King Zhou is referred to as "the fellow Zhou (who outrages the benevolent and righteous)."

124. Boyi and Shuqi, known for their wisdom, were brothers of the early Zhou era. See *Mencius* 2A:9; Ssu-ma Ch'ien (Sima Qian), *Records of the Historian*, 11–15; and note 61.

125. Mencius said that Boyi was a pure one among the sages (*Mencius* 5B:1).

126. *Analects* 6:16.

127. Ch'eng Hao, "Selected Sayings," in *Source Book*, trans. Chan, 535. The quote is from the *Complete Works of the Cheng Brothers*, where it is recorded that "a gentleman rectifies the inner heart by having reverence and the exterior becomes moral by having rightness" (Cheng Hao, *Yi shu*, in *Er Cheng quanshu*, chap. 5, 278).

128. The word *kūjaku* is commonly used for the Hinayana type of nirvana.

129. *Mushoju* (nonabiding) is a state of mind free from any thought of attachment.

130. *Analects* 12:10.

131. *Analects* 7:24. Confucius highlighted four subjects in his teaching: culture, moral conduct, loyalty, and faithfulness.

132. "Scholars of the Way" refers to the Neo-Confucians of the Song dynasty.

133. *Analects* 1:2.

134. "The Way of the superior man may be compared to traveling to a distant place: one must start from the nearest point. It may be compared to ascending a height: one must start from below" ("Doctrine of the Mean," in *Source Book*, trans. Chan, 102).

135. *Zhuzi yulei*, chap. 139, 1480. A Chan priest of the Tang, Zhaozhou

Congshen, said: "Sit for twenty or thirty years to plumb principle. If not en-lightened, cut off the head of an old priest."

136. Ibid., chap. 115, 4411. After the Tang period, the phrase was frequently used by Chan priests. This saying is recorded in Dahui Zonggao, *Biyan lu* (*Blue Cliff Records*).

137. Ibid., chap. 83, 3421.

138. This phrase appears in Zhou Dunyi's "Explanation of the Diagram of the Supreme Ultimate," but not in *Huayan fajie guan* (*Huayan View of the Realm of the Dharmas*), by Dushun (557–640), the founder of the Huayan school of Buddhism. See Zhu Xi, *Reflections on Things at Hand*, 5n.2.

139. This assertion alludes to why Zhu accepted Zhou's use of the Diagram of the Supreme Ultimate to explain cosmology, namely *taiji* and *wuji*.

140. The phrase is used by Cheng Yi in his preface to *Yiquan yizhuan* (*Commentary on the Classic of Changes*) ("Selected Sayings," in *Source Book*, trans. Chan, 570n.124). Chan notes that the first half of this phrase is attrib-uted to Cheng Guan (ca. 760–838), but it does not actually appear in his writ-ing. Chan suggests that the saying was common among both Buddhists and Confucians by the eleventh century.

141. Cheng Guan, the fourth patriarch of the Huayan sect and the author of *Huayan jing shu* (*Commentary on the Huayan Sutra*), was said to have been the most scholarly priest of the Tang period.

142. *Analects* 4:7.

143. The Cheng brothers said: "The Way is open to all" (*Er Cheng quanshu*, vol. 40).

144. *Analects* 12:20. In replying to Zizhang, Confucius said that a man who tries to win fame pretends to be benevolent, but his conduct is contrary to his outward benevolence. Nevertheless, he is self-assured and never doubts himself. Here he is contrasting being famous with being influential.

145. "Great Appendix," in *Book of Changes*, trans. Legge, 348.

146. "Explanation of the Divination Signs" states: "The Way of Heaven is defined as yin and yang; The Way of Earth is defined as hard and soft" (*Book of Changes*, trans. Legge, 423).

147. "The Great Appendix" says: "Heaven is high, earth is low; thus the Creative and the Receptive are determined" (*Book of Changes*, trans. Legge, 348).

148. "Explanation of the Divination Signs," in *Book of Changes*, trans. Legge, 423.

149. During the Han period, yin was related to the idea of femaleness and yang came to connote maleness. The *Book of Changes*, in "Appended Judgments," says: "Male and female energies are joined and this causes growth in all things."

150. "Explanation of the Divination Signs," in *Book of Changes*, trans. Legge, 423.

151. *Er Cheng quanshu*, vol. 12. Ekken disagrees with the Cheng brothers' interpretation of yin and yang as being below form.

152. The *Book of Changes*, in "Appended Judgments," says: "Yin and yang are all below form."

153. "The Sage" refers to Confucius.

154. "Two forms" refers to yin and yang. See "Appended Judgments," in *Book of Changes*, trans. Legge.

155. Chan translates this passage: "The Ultimate of Non-being and also the Great Ultimate (T'ai-chi)" (Chou Tun-i [Zhou Dunyi], "Explanation of the Diagram of the Great Ultimate," in *Source Book*, trans. Chan, 463). I have chosen to translate *wuji* as "nonfinite" and *taiji* as "Supreme Ultimate." Joseph Adler translates these terms as "Non-Polar" and "Supreme Polarity" (Zhou Dunyi, "Explanation of the Diagram of the Supreme Polarity," in *Sources of Chinese Tradition*, ed. de Bary and Bloom, 1:673).

156. *Zhuzi wenji*, SBBY, 36:9b.

157. *Laozi*, in *Source Book*, trans. Chan, 160.

158. Zhu Xi says in this work: "The terms *wuji* and *taiji* simply explain that principle exists without form" (*Zhuzi yulei*, chap. 94, 4904).

159. *Lu Jiuyuan ji*, vol. 2.

160. "Appended Judgments," in *Book of Changes*, trans. Legge.

161. The reference is to Confucius in "Appended Judgments," in *Book of Changes*.

162. *Lu Jiuyuan ji*, vol. 2.

163. Zhu Zifa (Zhu Zhen, 1072–1138) was a Confucian of the Northern Song period.

164. Mu Bozhang (Mu Xiu, 979–1032) and Chen Xiyi (Chen Tuan, ca. 906–989) were Daoists of the Northern Song period. For accounts of their lives, see *Sung Biographies*, ed. Franke, 2:793–794, 120–123.

165. *Laozi*, in *Source Book*, trans. Chan, 154.

166. There is actually no phrase corresponding to "the nonfinite and also the Supreme Ultimate" in the *Huayan fajie guan*. See Zhu Xi, *Reflections on Things at Hand*, 5n.2.

167. Here, too, Ekken is mistaken. See ibid.

168. *Laozi,* in *Source Book,* trans. Chan, 139.

169. Ibid., 160.

170. Wang Ziquan was a Confucian scholar of the early Qing. The quotation is from his book *Discussion on an Explanation of the Diagram of the Supreme Ultimate.*

171. Shouya was a Chan priest of the Northern Song period. Details about him are unknown.

172. Zhu Xi stated: "I think the excellence of Zhou's teachings lies in the Diagram. All the words in *Penetrating the Classic of Changes* are to develop the abstruse meaning of the Diagram" (*Zhuzi wenji,* SBBY, 75:18a). Thus Zhu Xi's position differs from that of Ekken, who separated the Diagram from *Penetrating the Classic of Changes* and regarded "An Explanation of the Diagram of the Supreme Ultimate" as an unfinished manuscript from Zhou's early years.

173. Ekken read Hao's text at age seventy and was confirmed in his reservations about Zhu Xi's metaphysics and affirmed his interest in the philosophy of *qi.* See Okada Takehiko, "Practical Learning in the Chu Hsi School: Yamazaki Ansai and Kaibara Ekken," in *Principle and Practicality: Essays in Neo-Confucianim and Practical Learning,* ed. Wm. Theodore de Bary and Irene Bloom (New York: Columbia University Press, 1979), 266, 288.

174. Chen Tuan was a Daoist of the Northern Song period who, according to tradition, lived at the foot of Mount Hua and practiced "ecstatic sleep." Zhou Dunyi reportedly knew of him and derived ideas about the concept of *taiji* from him.

175. Hu Wengong (Hu Su, 996–1067) was a Confucian of the Northern Song period.

176. Runzhou is located in present-day Jiangsu Province.

177. Zhang Jingfu (Zhang Shi, 1133–1180) was a scholar of the Southern Song period and a friend of Zhu Xi. The source of the attributed quotation is unknown.

178. Hao Jing (1558–1639), *Shixi xinzhi* (Jinan: Qi-Lu shushe chubanshe, 1997), vol. 6. However, the last sentence is a summary of the original, which states: "Most [philosophical] Confucians are refined and lofty. They are, of course, very wise. However, a Chan flavor pervades their scholarly style. This is not the correct transmission of the teaching of Confucius and Mencius."

179. *Zhuzi yulei,* chap. 1, 139.

180. Ibid., chap. 1, 144.

181. *Analects* 12:1.

182. *Mencius* 4A:9.

183. *Er Cheng quanshu*, chap. 2, 36.

184. *Zhuzi yulei*, chap. 41, 2303. For a biography of Yang Shi (1053–1135), see *Sung Biographies*, ed. Franke, 2:1226–1230.

185. Lü Dalin, *Inscription of Disciplining Oneself*, in *Song Yuan xue'an [Anthology of Philosophers of the Song and Yuan]*, SBBY, 31:8a. For an account of his life, see *Sung Biographies*, ed. Franke, 2:739–741.

186. In *Western Inscription*, Zhang Zai stressed that human beings are one with all creation and that ethics should be united with cosmic order. See Zhang Zai, "The 'Western Inscription,'" in *Sources of Chinese Tradition*, ed. de Bary and Bloom, 1:682–684.

187. Zhu Xi, *Lunyu jizhu [Commentary on the Analects]* (Taipei: Zhonghua congshu weiyuanhui, 1958), 7:216.

188. Wang Mang (45 B.C.E–23 C.E.), a Han politician, usurped the throne of the Han dynasty and established the Xin dynasty; after fifteen years on the throne, he himself was overthrown. See *Han shu*, chap. 99.

189. Tai Bo, an uncle of King Wen of the Zhou, renounced his right of succession to the throne in favor of his brother. Confucius said: "Of Tai Bo it should be said that he is outstanding in virtue. No less than three times he renounced the sovereignty of all things under Heaven, but no one praised him" (*Analects* 8:1).

190. In their youth, the Cheng brothers studied under the supervision of Zhou Dunyi.

191. *Analects* 13:24.

192. *Analects* 12:1.

193. *Analects* 12:20.

194. *Analects* 12:20: "He who achieves a deep understanding is by nature straightforward and loves rightness. He examines others' words, observes their expressions and bears in mind the necessity of being humble to others. Such a person will certainly achieve a deep understanding, whether employed by the state or by a ruling family."

195. *Analects* 14:37.

196. Kong Yingda (576–648). See *Shangshu zhushu [Commentaries on the Classic of Documents]*, SBBY, 12:8b.

197. Ibid., vol. 6.

198. *Zhuzi wenji*, SBBY, 59:17a.

199. Zhu Xi was critical of the position of Yang Shi and Lü Dalin. He said their explanations were too lofty and lose the meaning of the sages. Ekken found this unreasonable.

200. In *Guoyu*, it is said: "Caution is something which can protect virtue" (chap. 3, 98). Ekken replaced "caution" with "reverence."

201. In *Zuo's Commentary on the Spring and Autumn Annals*, it is stated: "Reverence is something which can foster virtue. If one reveres well, one certainly attains virtue which regulates the people" (*The Ch'un Ts'ew with the Tso Chuen*, vol. 5 of *The Chinese Classics*, trans. James Legge [Hong Kong: Hong Kong University Press, 1960], 223).

202. "Doctrine of the Mean," in *Source Book*, trans. Chan, 108.

203. In *Daxue huowen* (*Questions and Answers on the Great Learning*), Zhu Xi states: "The practice of reverence is the first meaning for the Gate of the Sages. It must be practiced thoroughly without any interruption" (Kinsei kanseki sōkan, shisō sanben, chap. 5, 4). For Neo-Confucians, the practice of reverence should be based on awe and obedience to the Heavenly Principle, which consequently leads one to serious, solemn appearance and attitude. The practice, however, tended to emphasize only seriousness and severity and result in the formation of a cold, inhumane personality. Ekken strongly opposed this tendency toward severity in the practice of reverence.

204. Ibid.

205. *Analects* 14:45.

206. *Mencius* 6A:8: "Confucius said, 'Hold on to it and it will remain; let go of it, and it will disappear. One never knows the time it comes or goes, neither does one know the direction.' It is perhaps the heart this refers to."

207. "People who flatter Zhu Xi" refers to the scholars of the Yamazaki Ansai school.

208. *Analects* 12:10.

209. "Sincerity is the Way of heaven. To think how to be sincere is the Way of man" ("Doctrine of the Mean," in *Source Book*, trans. Chan, 107).

210. "Explanation of the Words and Sentences," in *Book of Changes*, trans. Legge.

211. *Er Cheng quanshu*, vol. 53.

212. "The Canon of Yao," in *Shu King*, trans. Legge, 15.

213. "The Canon of Shun," in ibid., 29.

214. "Counsels of the Great Yu," in ibid., 52.

215. "Long Manifested," in *The She King*, vol. 4 of *The Chinese Classics*, ed. James Legge (Hong Kong: Hong Kong University Press, 1960), 640.

216. "King Wen," in ibid., 429.

217. "Wu Wang Jiangzu," in *Da Dai liji* [*Elder Dai's Record of Rites*], in *Kungzi wenhua daquan* (Jinan: Shandong youyi shushe, 1991), 6:1b, 120.

218. Tai Gong rendered distinguished service to King Wu and King Wen of the Zhou.

219. *Analects* 14:45.

220. "Summary of the Rites," in *Li Chi: Book of Rites*, trans. James Legge (New Hyde Park, N.Y.: University Books, 1967), 1:61.

221. *Er Cheng quanshu*, 12:393.

222. Confucius said: "In Heaven there are not two suns. For the people there are not two kings" (*Mencius* 5A:4).

223. *Analects* 17:12.

224. This is the premise of the "Doctrine of the Mean," in *Source Book*, trans. Chan, 107–110.

225. "Explanation of the Divination Signs," in *Book of Changes*, trans. Legge.

226. "Wisdom, humaneness and courage, these three are the universal virtues, the way by which they are practiced is one" ("Doctrine of the Mean," in *Source Book*, trans. Chan, 105).

227. Zhu Xi, "On the Substance of the Way," in *Reflections on Things at Hand*, 5–8.

228. "The Little Min" (Xiao min), in *She King*, trans. Legge, 333.

229. "Long Manifested," in ibid., 433.

230. "Doctrine of the Mean," in *Source Book*, trans. Chan, 98.

231. "Di zi zhi," in *Guanzi* [*Collection of the Words of Guan Zhong and His Students*], Kokuyaku kanbun taisei, keishi shibu (Tokyo: Tōyō bunka kyōkai, 1955), 18:597. Guan Zhong (d. 645 B.C.E.) was a statesman of the Spring and Autumn period and consolidated the power of the Ji kingdom.

232. *Zhuzi yulei*, vol. 15.

233. Quoted in Zhu Xi, *Reflections on Things at Hand*, 57. Sun Simiao (601–682), the author of *Qianjin fang*, was a Daoist hermit who lived during the Tang.

234. *Mencius* 2A:2.

235. Ibid.

236. *Analects* 7:4: "In his leisure hours, Confucius was free and easy and his expression alert and cheerful."

237. Chang Tsai (Zhang Zai), "Great Harmony," in *Source Book*, trans. Chan, 501.

238. Luo, *Knowledge Painfully Acquired*, 127.

239. *Laozi*, in *Source Book*, trans. Chan, 156.

240. *Chuang Tzu: Basic Writings*, trans. Burton Watson (New York: Columbia University Press, 1996), 135.

241. The Cheng brothers and Zhu Xi interpreted the words in the *Classic of Changes* ("yin and yang are the Way") as "the source for yin and yang are the Way." In this interpretation, yin and yang are separated from principle, and principle is thus regarded as something empty and void.

242. "Doctrine of the Mean," in *Source Book*, trans. Chan, 110.

243. Luo, *Knowledge Painfully Acquired*, 173.

244. This may be a misreading of Zhu Xi and Lü Zuqian as seen in *Reflections on Things at Hand*, in which Lü indicated that "if the shadow proceeds accordingly, ascending from low to the high and going from the near to the far, he will probably not miss the aim of this anthology" (3).

245. *Laozi*, in *Source Book*, trans. Chan, 152.

246. "Appended Judgments," in *Book of Changes*, trans. Legge.

247. In the *Classic of Changes*, it says that the Supreme Ultimate refers to one primal material force before a distinction is made between Heaven and Earth. See *I Ching*, trans. Wilhelm and Baynes, 318.

248. "Appended Judgments," in *Book of Changes*, trans. Legge.

249. Ibid.

250. Ibid.

251. In chapter 2 of the *Classified Conversations of Zhu Xi*, it is written: "Question: Which exists first, principle or material force? Answer: Principle has never been separated from material force. However, principle is above form. On the other hand, material force is below form. Hence when spoken of as being above or below form, how is there a difference of priority and posteriority?" (*Zhuzi yulei*, 142).

252. *Laozi*, in *Source Book*, trans. Chan, 152.

253. It is said that Zhou Dunyi learned these ideas from a Northern Song Buddhist monk, Shouya. These ideas assume the existence of an Absolute beyond concrete phenomena, a position with which Ekken disagreed.

254. Material force has power that creates all things through its orderly operation, and the order itself is principle. Hence Ekken asserts principle also has a power that creates all things.

255. Postulating that material force and principle are originally one, Ekken concluded that material force cannot be created from principle.

256. Liu Shuwen, whose birth name was Liu Yi (awarded the *jinshi* degree in 1193), was a friend of Zhu Xi. The *jinshi* degree was awarded upon the successful completion of a special imperial examination.

幕府	J. *bakufu*, shogunal government
萬物一體	J. *banbutsu ittai*, C. *wanwu yiti*, forming one body with all things
本	C. *ben*, J. *hon*, root, fundamental, essential
本體	C. *benti*, J. *hontai*, the essential or fundamental root
本心	C. *benxin*, J. *honshin*, fundamental mind-and-heart
誠	C. *cheng*, J. *makoto*, sincerity, integrity, self-realization, actualization of the true creative potential of human affairs, even of the cosmos
程明道	Cheng Mingdao (Cheng Hao 程顥)
程伊川	Cheng Yichuan (Cheng Yi 程頤)
誠意	C. *chengyi*, J. *seiri*, making one's intention sincere
筑前	Chikuzen
大名	J. *daimyō*, leader of a feudal domain
道	C. *dao* or *tao*, J. *dō*, the Way, a path, way of proper conduct, to lead through, matrix of all the things and events of the cosmos
道德	C. *daode*, J. *dōtoku*, virtue
道理	C. *daoli*, J. *dōri*, the Way and its principles
道學	C. *daoxue*, J. *dōgaku*, learning of the Way
大學	C. *Daxue*, J. *Daigaku*, *The Great Learning*

德	C. *de*, J. *toku*, virtue, potency, excellence, the power of virtue, that which has ethical power
董仲舒	Dong Zhongshu
而	C. *er*, and also, in turn
福岡	Fukuoka
格物	C. *gewu*, J. *kakubutsu*, examination of things and events
公	C. *gong*, J. *kō*, public, public good, the public sphere of activity
恭敬和樂	C. *gongjing hele*, J. *kyōkei waraku*, reverence and harmony
藩	J. *han*, provincial domain
和	C. *he*, J. *wa*, harmony of a situation or person
本草綱目	J. *Honzō komoku*, C. *Bencao gangmu*, *Index of Materia Medica*
化	C. *hua*, J. *kasu*, to transform utterly such that A becomes B
伊藤仁齊	Itō Jinsai
敬	C. *jing*, J. *kei*, reverence, respect, the concentration of reverence on the moral path
近思錄	C. *Jinsilu*, J. *Kinshiroku*, *Reflections on Things at Hand*
居敬	C. *jujing*, J. *kyokei*, abiding in reverence
君子	C. *junzi*, J. *kunshi*, gentleman; exemplary person; originally meant the son of a prince or a nobleman; second in virtue only to the sage
儒者	J. *jusha*, literatus; scholar
受用の學	J. *juyō no gaku*, C. *shouyong xue*, preserved in the heart and carried out in action
貝原益軒	Kaibara Ekken (also Kaibara Ekiken)
氣の思想	J. *ki no shisō*, philosophy of material force
氣學	J. *kigaku*, C. *qixue*, school of material force
木下順庵	Kinoshita Jun'an
困知記	C. *Kunzhiji*, *Knowledge Painfully Acquired*
理	C. *li*, J. *ri*, principle that orders all things, persons, and events; form, pattern, norm, the defining pattern or principle of the cosmos
禮	C. *li*, J. *ri*, ritual, civility, proper social order, customs, etiquette, ritual propriety
立	C. *li*, J. *ritsu*, to establish, set up, to make firm (in virtue and conduct)

李時珍	Li Shizhen
良知	C. *liangzhi*, J. *ryōchi*, innate knowledge of the good
理一分殊	C. *liyi fenshu*, J. *riichi bunshu*, principle is one; its manifestations are many
陸象山	Lu Xiangshan
論語	C. *Lunyu*, J. *Rongō*, *Analects*
羅欽順	Luo Qinshun
丸山真男	Maruyama Masao
孟子	C. Mengzi, J. *Mōshi*, Mencius
源了圜	Minamoto Ryōen
明明德	C. *ming ming de*, J. *meimeitoku*, manifesting clear character or virtue
無用の學	J. *muyō no gaku*, C. *wuyongxue*, useless learning
長崎	Nagasaki
中江藤樹	Nakae Tōju
農業全書	J. *Nōgyō zensho, Compendium on Agriculture*
氣	C. *qi* or *ch'i*, J. *ki*, material force, vital force, vital energy, matter-energy, the dynamic element of all that is
情	C. *qing*, J. *jō*, emotions, feelings, desires, the developed nature of a person
窮理	C. *qiongli*, J. *kyūri*, exploring principle
人	C. *ren*, J. *jin*, human being
仁	C. *ren*, J. *jin*, humaneness, humanity, human-heartedness, benevolence, first of the Confucian virtues, love
人道	C. *rendao*, J. *jindō*, human Way, Way to be human
人倫	C. *renlun*, J. *jinrin*, human relations; morality
人欲	C. *renyu*, J. *ninjō*, human emotion, human passions, passionate human feelings or emotions
理學	J. *rigaku*, C. *lixue*, school of principle
儒	C. *ru*, J. *ju*, scholar, ritual specialist, Chinese term for a Confucian; also 儒學者, 儒者
鎖國	J. *sakoku*, closed country
士, 侍	J. *samurai*
參勤交代	J. sankin kōtai, alternate attendance system
性理	J. *seiri*, C. *xingli*, life principle

神	C. *shen*, J. *kami*, spirit, spiritual, numinous
伸	C. *shen*, J. *shin*, extension
身	C. *shen*, J. *shin*, self, person, body
慎	C. *shen*, J. *tsutsushimu*, having reverent mindfulness
生	C. *sheng*, J. *sei*, life giving
生生	C. *sheng sheng*, J. *sei sei*, production and reproduction, fecundity
聖人	C. *shengren*, J. *seijin*, sage, the perfected person
實	C. *shi*, J. *jitsu*, substantial, real, practical
史記	C. *Shiji*, *Record of the Historian*
實學	C. *shixue*, J. *jitsugaku*, practical learning
恕	C. *shu*, J. jo, reciprocity, mutuality, empathy
私	C. *si*, J. *shi*, private, personal
四端	C. *siduan*, J. *shitan*, four roots or seeds of virtue
私欲	C. *siyu*, J. *shiyoku*, selfish desires
大疑錄	J. *Taigiroku, Record of Great Doubts*
太和	C. *taihe*, J. *taiwa*, Great Harmony
太極	C. *taiji*, J. *taikyoku*, Supreme Polarity or Supreme Ultimate
太極圖說	C. *Taiji tushuo*, J. *Taikyoku zusetsu*, Diagram of the Supreme Ultimate
太虛	C. *taixu*, J. *taikyo*, Great Vacuity, the origin of the universe
唐君毅	Tang Junyi (Tang Chün-I)
體	C. *ti*, J. *tai*, substance, body, essence
天	C. *tian*, J. *ten*, Heaven; sky, the blue sky, the high god of the Zhou people
天道	C. *tiandao*, J. *tendō*, the Way of Heaven
天地	C. *tiandi*, J. *tenchi*, Heaven and Earth, nature
天機	C. *tianji*, J. *tenki*, workings of Heaven
天理	C. *tianli*, J. *tenri*, Heavenly principle, ultimate principle or norm of the good or perfect
天命	C. *tianming*, J. *tenmei*, Mandate of Heaven
天下	C. *tianxia*, J. *tenka*, All under Heaven, everyone and everything
體用	C. *tiyong*, J. *taiyō*, substance and function
德川	Tokugawa
王陽明	C. Wang Yangming, J. Ōyōmei
未發	C. *weifa*, not yet manifested

無	C. *wu*, J. *mu*, nonbeing, nothingness
五常	C. *wuchang*, J. *gojō*, five constant virtues: humaneness, righteousness, ritual/civility, wisdom or discernment, and faithfulness
無極	C. *wuji*, J. *mukyoku*, nonfinite, the Ultimate of Nonpolarity, the infinite, nonbeing
孝	C. *xiao*, J. *kō*, filial piety, filiality, deference, respect
小人	C. *xiaoren*, J. *shōjin*, petty person
西銘	C. *Ximing, Western Inscription*
信	C. *xin*, J. *shin*, faithfulness, honesty, integrity of thought, word, and action; virtue of friendship, credibility
心	C. *xin*, J. *shin*, mind-and-heart, heart-mind; seat of the intelligence; most refined aspect of the vital force
性	C. *xing*, J. *sei*, human nature, natural tendencies
形而上	C. *xingershang*, J. *keijijō*, what is above form; incorporeal
形而下	C. *xingerxia*, J. *keijika*, what is below form; corporeal
新民	C. *xinmin*, J. *shinmin*, renew the people
心學	C. *xinxue*, J. *shingaku*, learning of the mind-and-heart
修	C. *xiu*, J. *shō*, cultivation, discipline
修身	C. *xiushen*, J. *shōshin*, self-cultivation
學	C. *xue*, J. *gaku*, study
山鹿素行	Yamaga Sokō
山崎闇齊	Yamazaki Ansai
養生術	C. *yangsheng shu*, J. *yōjō no jutsu*, nourishing of life
義	C. *yi*, J. *gi*, righteousness, moral appropriateness
易	C. *yi*, J. *i*, change or transformation
意	C. *yi*, J. *i*, intentions, motivations
李退溪	Yi T'oegye
李栗谷	Yi Yulgok
已發	C. *yifa*, already manifested (as certain qualities or objects and events)
易經	C. *Yijing, Classic of Changes, Book of Changes*
陰陽	C. *yinyang*, yin-yang forces; positive and negative, light and dark, female and male
養生訓	J. *Yōjōkun*, C. *Yangshengxun, Precepts on Health Care*
用	C. *yong*, J. *yō*, function, use, operation

有用學	C. *youyongxue*, J. *yūyō no gaku*, useful learning
欲	C. *yu*, J. *yoku*, desire, passion, emotion
元	C. *yuan*, J. *gen*, origination
元亨利真	C. *yuan, heng, li, zhen*, origin, flourishing, advantage, firmness
張載	Zhang Zai
正	C. *zheng*, J. *sei*, rectification, to make correct, to bring order
正心	C. *zhengxin*, J. *seishin*, to establish or rectify the mind-and-heart
知	C. *zhi*, J. *chi*, knowledge, intelligence, discernment, wisdom
志	C. *zhi*, J. *shi*, will, fortitude of character
至善	C. *zhishan*, J. *shizen*, resting in the highest good
致知	C. *zhizhi*, J. *chichi*, the extension of knowledge or the capacity to know
中	C. *zhong*, J. *chū*, centrality, the mean, equilibrium, being centered in proper virtue
忠	C. *zhong*, J. *chū*, loyalty, being completely committed
忠恕	C. *zhongshu*, J. *chūjo*, conscientiousness and altruism
中庸	C. *zhongyong*, *The Mean, Centrality and Commonality*, title of one of the Four Books; locus for achieving harmony
周敦頤	Zhou Dunyi
朱熹	C. Zhu Xi, J. Shushi.
主忠信	C. *zhu zhongxin*, J. *shuchōshin*, making loyalty and faithfulness the master
自得	C. *zide*, J. *jitoku*, getting it for oneself; self-attainment
自然	C. *ziran*, J. *shizen*, spontaneity, uncontrived action, complete freedom

BOOKS AND ARTICLES IN JAPANESE

Abe Yoshio. *Jukyō no hensen to genkyō* [*The Development and the Present Situation of Confucianism*]. Tokyo: Kazankai, 1977.

———. *Nihon Shushigaku to Chōsen* [*The Japanese Zhu Xi School and Korea*]. Tokyo: Tokyo Daigaku shuppankai, 1971.

Aoki Yoshinori. "Kaibara Ekken no 'Shinju heikō fusō hairon'" [A Discussion of Similarities and Differences between Shinto and Confucianism]. *Shigaku zasshi* 50, no. 1 (1939): 223–239.

Bitō Masahide. *Nihon hōken shisōshi kenkyū* [*Studies in the History of Thought in Japanese Feudalism*]. Tokyo: Aoki shoten, 1961.

Hongō Takamori and Fukaya Katsumi, eds. *Kinsei shisōron* [*Discussions of Premodern Japanese Thought*]. Tokyo: Yūhikaku, 1981.

Inoue Tadashi. *Kaibara Ekken*. Tokyo: Yoshikawa kōbunkan, 1963.

———. "Kaibara Ekken no 'Dōjimon higo' ni tsuite" [Concerning Kaibara Ekken's Critique of "Boy's Questions"]. *Kyūshū Daigaku kenkyū hōkoku* (1977): 121–177.

Inoue Tadashi and Araki Kengo, eds. *Kaibara Ekken, Muro Kyūsō*. Nihon shisō taikei, vol. 34. Tokyo: Iwanami shoten, 1970.

Inoue Tetsujirō. *Nihon Shushigakuha no tetsugaku* [*The Philosophy of the Zhu Xi School in Japan*]. Tokyo: Fuzanbō, 1926.

Inoue Tetsujirō et al. *Nihon tetsugaku zensho* [*Collected Works in Japanese Philosophy*]. Vol. 3, *Jukyōhen*; vol. 9, *Jukyōka no shizenkan*. Tokyo: Daiichi shobō, 1937.

Irizawa Sōju. *Kaibara Ekken*. Nihon kyōiku sentetsu sōsho. Tokyo: Bunkyō shoin, 1954.

Ishii Shirō. *Kinsei buke shisō* [*Premodern Samurai Thought*]. Nihon shisō taikei, vol. 27. Tokyo: Iwanami shoten, 1974.

Ishikawa Matsutarō, ed. *Kaibara Ekken, Muro Kyūsō shū*. Sekai kyōiku hōten. Nihon kyōiku hen, vol. 3. Tokyo: Tamagawa Daigaku shuppanbu, 1968.

Itō Tomonobu, ed. *Shinshiroku* [*Record of Careful Thoughts*]. Tokyo: Kōdansha, 1966.

Iwabashi Junsei. *Dainihon rinri shisō hattatsushi* [*A History of the Development of Ethical Thought in Japan*]. Vol. 1. Tokyo: Meguro shoten, 1915.

Kaibara Ekken. *Ekken jikkun* [*Ekken's Ten Moral Treatises*]. Edited by Tsukamoto Tetsuzō. 2 vols. Tokyo: Yūhōdō shoten, 1927.

——. *Ekken zenshū* [*The Collected Works of Kaibara Ekken*]. Edited by Ekkenkai. 8 vols. Tokyo: Ekken zenshū kankōbu, 1910–1911.

——. *Kaibara Ekken shū* [*Collection of Kaibara Ekken's Works*]. Edited by Takigawa Masajirō. Kinsei shakai keizai gakusetsu taikei, vol. 10. Tokyo: Seibundō shinkōsha, 1939.

——. *Yamato zokkun* [*Precepts for Daily Life in Japan*]. Tokyo: Kiyomizu Kakujirō, 1967.

Kinugasa Yasuki. *Kinsei Jugaku shisōshi no kenkyū* [*Studies in the History of Premodern Confucian Thought*]. Tokyo: Hōsei Daigaku shuppankyoku, 1976.

Komoguchi Isao and Okada Takehiko. *Andō Seian, Kaibara Ekken*. Tokyo: Meitoku shuppansha, 1985.

Kumida Yoshio. "Kaibara Ekken no yōjōkan no tokushitsu" [Special Characteristics of Kaibara Ekken's Views on Health Care]. *Shisō* 528 (1968): 82–94.

Kyūshū shiryō kankōkai, ed. *Kyūshū shiryō sōsho*. Kyūshū: Kyūshū shiryō kankōkai, 1964. [Includes Sonken nikkiryaku; Kanbun nikki; Enpō shichinen nikki; Nikki (5 and 6); Kyoka nikki; Zakki; Shokanshū; Kaibara Ekken ate shokan; Ganko mokuroku; Atsunobu isei yōzaiki]

Maki Katsumi. "Kaibara Ekken no ichigenki ni tsuite" [Concerning Kaibara Ekken's Monism of Ch'i]. *Shinagaku kenkyū* (1960): 217–222.

——. "Kaibara Ekken no uchūkan ni tsuite" [Concerning Kaibara Ekken's View of the Universe]. *Shinagaku kenkyū* (1966): 42–49.

Matsuda Michio, ed. *Kaibara Ekken.* Vol. 14, *Nihon no meicho.* Tokyo: Chūō kōronsha, 1969.

Minamoto Ryōen. *Kinsei shoki jitsugaku shisō no kenkyū* [*Studies in Practical Learning at the Beginning of the Premodern Era*]. Tokyo: Sōbunsha, 1980.

——. *Tokugawa gōri shisō no keifu* [*The Lineage of Rational Thought in the Tokugawa Period*]. Tokyo: Chūō kōronsha, 1972.

——. "Tokugawa jidai ni okeru gōriteki shi-i no hatten" [The Development of Rationalistic Thought in the Tokugawa Period]. *Kokoro*, no. 21 (1968): 56–63.

——. *Tokugawa shisō shōshi* [*A Short History of Tokugawa Thought*]. Tokyo: Chūō kōronsha, 1973.

Morishita Sanao. "Kaibara Ekken no tendō shisō" [The Idea of the Heavenly Way of Kaibara Ekken]. *Rekishi to chiri* 17, no. 5 (1925): 412–420.

Naramoto Tatsuya and Kinugasa Yasuki. *Edo jidai no shisō* [*Edo Period Thought*]. Tokyo: Tokuma shoten, 1966.

Saegusa Hiroto, ed. *Nihon tetsugaku shisō zensho* [*Collected Works in Japanese Philosophical Thought*]. Vol. 7, *Gakumon hen;* vol. 14, *Jukyōhen.* Tokyo: Heibonsha, 1957.

Sagara Tōru. *Kinsei Nihon ni okeru Jukyō undō no keifu* [*The Lineage of the Movement of Confucianism in Premodern Japan*]. Tokyo: Risōsha, 1965.

Sagara Tōru et al. *Edo no shisōkatachi* [*Thinkers in the Edo Period*]. Tokyo: Kenkyūsha, 1979.

Saitō Shigeta, ed. *Jinseikun: Kaibara Ekken "Kadōkun" o yomu* [*A Reading of Kaibara Ekken's "Precepts for the Way of the Family"*]. Tokyo: Mikasa shoten, 1984.

Saitō Tokutarō. *Kinsei Jurin hennen shi* [*Chronological Account of Japanese Confucianists of Premodern Times*]. Osaka: Zenkoku shobō, 1943.

Takada Shinji. *Nihon Jugakushi* [*A History of Japanese Confucianism*]. Tokyo: Chinin shokan, 1941.

Tsuboi Hideo. *Nihon no dōtoku shisō* [*Japanese Moral Thought*]. Tokyo: Bunka sōgō shuppansha, 1981.

Tsuda Sōkichi. *Jukyō no kenkyū* [*Studies in Confucianism*]. Tokyo: Iwanami shoten, 1956.

Tsuji Tetsuo. "Kaibara Ekken no gakumon to hōhō" [Kaibara Ekken's Learning and Methodology]. *Shisō* 11, no. 605 (1974): 57–71.

Tsujimoto Masashi. *Kinsei kyōiku shisō shi no kenkyū* [*Studies in Early Modern Educational Thought*]. Kyoto: Shibunkaku shuppan, 1990.

——. Kyōiku shisutemu no naka no shintai: Kaibara Ekken ni okeru gakushū to shintai" [The Body in the Education System: Learning and the Body in Kaibara Ekken]. *Edo no shisō* 6 (1997).

Tsukamoto Tetsuzō, ed. *Kaibara Ekken*. Tokyo: Yūhōdō shoten, 1927.

Watanabe Shōichi. *Nihon kinsei dōtoku shisōshi* [*A History of Moral Thought in the Premodern Era in Japan*]. Tokyo: Sōbunsha, 1961.

Yajima Genryō, ed. *Kangakusha denki sakuin* [*An Index of Biographies of Japanese Scholars of the Chinese Classics*]. Sendai: Tōhoku Daigaku fuzoku toshokan, 1970.

Yokoyama Toshio, ed. *Kaibara Ekken: Tenchi waraku no bunmeigaku* [*The Humanistic Study of the Harmony of the Universe*]. Tokyo: Heibonsha, 1995.

BOOKS IN WESTERN LANGUAGES

Arai Hakuseki. *Told Round a Brushwood Fire: The Autobiography of Arai Hakuseki*. Translated by Joyce Ackroyd. Princeton: Princeton University Press, 1980.

Armstrong, Robert Cornell. *Light from the East: Studies in Japanese Confucianism*. 1914. Reprint, New York: Gordon Press, 1974.

Bellah, Robert. *Imagining Japan: The Japanese Tradition and Its Modern Interpretation*. Berkeley: University of California Press, 2003.

——. *Tokugawa Religion: The Values of Pre-Industrial Japan*. Boston: Beacon Press, 1957.

Berthrong, John H., and Evelyn Nagai Berthrong. *Confucianism: A Short Introduction*. Oxford: Oneworld, 2000.

Bowers, John. *Western Medical Pioneers in Feudal Japan*. Baltimore: Johns Hopkins University Press, 1970.

Boxer, C. R. *The Christian Century in Japan, 1549–1650*. Berkeley: University of California Press, 1951.

Callicott, J. Baird, and Roger Ames, eds. *Nature in Asian Traditions of Thought*. Albany: State University of New York Press, 1989.

Chapple, Christopher Key, ed. *Ecological Prospects: Scientific, Religious, and Aesthetic Perspectives.* Albany: State University of New York Press, 1994.

Chan, Wing-tsit. *Chu Hsi: Life and Thought.* Hong Kong: Chinese University Press, 1987.

——. *Neo-Confucianism, Etc.: Essays by Wing-tsit Chan.* Compiled by Charles K. H. Chen. Hanover, N.H.: Oriental Society, 1969.

——, ed. *Chu Hsi and Neo-Confucianism.* Honolulu: University of Hawaii Press, 1986.

——, trans. and comp. *A Source Book in Chinese Philosophy.* Princeton: Princeton University Press, 1963.

Chen Beixi. *Neo-Confucian Terms Explained: The Pei-hsi tzu-i.* Translated by Wing-tsit Chan. New York: Columbia University Press, 1986.

Ching, Julia. *The Religious Thought of Chu Hsi.* Oxford: Oxford University Press, 2000.

Chow, Kai-wing, On-cho Ng, and John B. Henderson, eds. *Imagining Boundaries: Changing Confucian Doctrines, Texts, and Hermeneutics.* Albany: State University of New York Press, 1999.

de Bary, Wm. Theodore. *East Asia: The Great Dialogue.* Cambridge, Mass.: Harvard University Press, 1988.

——. *Learning for Oneself.* New York: Columbia University Press, 1991.

——. *The Liberal Tradition in China.* New York: Columbia University Press, 1983.

——. *The Message of the Mind in Neo-Confucianism.* New York: Columbia University Press, 1988.

——. *Neo-Confucian Orthodoxy and the Learning of the Mind-and-Heart.* New York: Columbia University Press, 1981.

——, ed. *Self and Society in Ming Thought.* New York: Columbia University Press, 1970.

——, ed. *The Unfolding of Neo-Confucianism.* New York: Columbia University Press, 1975.

de Bary, Wm. Theodore, and Irene Bloom, eds. *Principle and Practicality: Essays in Neo-Confucianism and Practical Learning.* New York: Columbia University Press, 1979.

——, eds. *Sources of Chinese Tradition.* 2nd ed. Vol. 1. New York: Columbia University Press, 1999.

de Bary, Wm. Theodore, and John W. Chaffee, eds. *Neo-Confucian Education: The Formative Stage*. Berkeley: University of California Press, 1989.

de Bary, Wm. Theodore, Carol Gluck, and Arthur E. Tiedemann, eds. *Sources of Japanese Tradition*. Vol. 2, *1600–2000*. 2nd ed. New York: Columbia University Press, 2005.

Dore, Ronald P. *Education in Tokugawa Japan*. Berkeley: University of California Press, 1965.

Elison, George. *Deus Destroyed: The Image of Christianity in Early Modern Japan*. Cambridge, Mass.: Harvard University Press, 1973.

Elman, Benjamin, John B. Duncan, and Herman Ooms, eds. *Rethinking Confucianism: Past and Present in China, Japan, Korea and Vietnam*. Los Angeles: UCLA Asian Pacific Monograph Series, 2002.

Fung Yu-lan. *A Short History of Chinese Philosophy*. New York: Free Press, 1948.

Gardner, Daniel. *Zhu Xi's Reading of the "Analects": Canon, Commentary and the Confucian Tradition*. New York: Columbia University Press, 2003.

Graf, Olaf. *Kaibara Ekiken*. Leiden: Brill, 1942.

Hall, David, and Roger Ames. *Thinking Through Confucius*. Albany: State University of New York Press, 1987.

The I Ching, or Book of Changes. Translated by Richard Wilhelm and, from the German, Cary F. Baynes. Bollingen Series 19. Princeton: Princeton University Press, 1967.

Ikegami, Eiko. *The Taming of the Samurai: Honorific Individualism and the Making of Modern Japan*. Cambridge, Mass.: Harvard University Press, 1995.

Jansen, Marius. *China in the Tokugawa World*. Cambridge, Mass.: Harvard University Press, 1992.

——, ed. *Changing Japanese Attitudes Toward Modernization*. Princeton: Princeton University Press, 1965.

Kaempfer, Engelbert. *The History of Japan, Together with a Description of the Kingdom of Siam, 1690–1692*. Translated by J. G. Scheuchzer. 3 vols. Glasgow: Maclehose, 1906.

Kaibara Ekken. "Onna Daigaku." Translated by Basil Hall Chamberlain. In *Japanese Things*. 1905. Reprint, Rutland, Vt.: Tuttle, 1971.

——. *The Way of Contentment*. Translated by Ken Hoshino. London: John Murray, 1913.

——. *Yōjōkun: Japanese Secret of Good Health*. Translated by Masao Kunihiro. Tokyo: Tokuma shoten, 1974.

Kalton, Michael, Oaksoot C. Kim, and Sung Bae Park. *The Four-Seven Debate: An Annotated Translation of the Most Famous Controversy in Korean Neo-Confucian Thought*. Albany: State University of New York Press, 1994.

Kasoff, Ira E. *The Thought of Chang Tsai (1020–1077)*. Cambridge: Cambridge University Press, 1984.

Kassel, Marleen. *Tokugawa Confucian Education: The Kangien Academy of Hirose Tansō (1783–1865)*. Albany: State University of New York Press, 1996.

Keene, Donald. *World Within Walls: Japanese Literature of the Pre-Modern Era, 1600–1867*. New York: Holt, Rinehart and Winston, 1976.

Kim, Yung Sik. *The Natural Philosophy of Chu Hsi, 1130–1200*. Philadelphia: American Philosophical Society, 2000.

Kirkwood, Kenneth B. *Renaissance in Japan: A Cultural Survey of the Seventeenth Century*. 1938. Reprint, Rutland, Vt.: Tuttle, 1970.

Kreiner, Josef, ed. *The Impact of Traditional Thought on Present-Day Japan*. Munich: Iudicium Verlag, 1996.

Legge, James, trans. *Book of Changes*. New York: Dover, 1963.

——, trans. *The Ch'un Ts'ew with the Tso Chuen*. Vol. 5 of *The Chinese Classics*. Hong Kong: Hong Kong University Press, 1960.

——, trans. *The Confucian Analects, the Great Learning, and the Doctrine of the Mean*. Vol. 1 of *The Chinese Classics*. Hong Kong: Hong Kong University Press, 1960.

——, trans. *Li Chi: Book of Rites*. 2 vols. New Hyde Park, N.Y.: University Books, 1967.

——, trans. *The She King [Shi-ching]*. Vol. 4 of *The Chinese Classics*. Hong Kong: Hong Kong University Press, 1960.

——, trans. *The Shu King [Shu-ching,]*. Vol. 3 of *The Chinese Classics*. Hong Kong: Hong Kong University Press, 1960.

Lidin, Olof. *The Life of Ogyū Sorai, a Tokugawa Confucian Philosopher*. Lund: Scandinavian Institute of Asian Studies, 1973.

Luo Qinshun. *Knowledge Painfully Acquired: The K'un-chih chi by Lo Ch'in-shun*. Translated by Irene Bloom. New York: Columbia University Press, 1987.

Maruyama, Masao. *Studies in the Intellectual History of Tokugawa Japan*. Translated by Mikiso Hane. Princeton: Princeton University Press, 1974.

McMullen, Ian James. *Idealism, Protest and "The Tale of Genji": The Confucian-ism of Kumazawa Banzan*. Oxford: Clarendon Press, 1999.

Mencius. *Mencius*. Translated by D. C. Lau. Harmondsworth: Penguin, 1970.

Miura Baien. *Deep Words: Miura Baien's System of Natural Philosophy*. Trans-lated by Rosemary Mercer. Leiden: Brill, 1991.

Najita, Tetsuo. *Visions of Virtue in Tokugawa Japan: The Kaitokudō Merchant Academy of Osaka*. Chicago: University of Chicago Press, 1987.

———, ed. *Readings in Tokugawa Thought*. 2nd ed. Select Papers, vol. 9. Chi-cago: Center for East Asian Studies, University of Chicago, 1994.

———, trans. *Tokugawa Political Writings*. Cambridge: Cambridge University Press, 1998.

Najita, Tetsuo, and Irwin Scheiner, eds. *Japanese Thought in the Tokugawa Pe-riod, 1600–1868: Methods and Metaphors*. Chicago: University of Chicago Press, 1978.

Nakai, Kate Wildman. *Shogunal Politics: Arai Hakuseki and the Premises of Tokugawa Rule*. Cambridge, Mass.: Council on East Asian Studies, Har-vard University, 1988.

Nakamura, Hajime. *A History of the Development of Japanese Thought from A.D. 592 to 1868*. Tokyo: Kokusai bunka shinkōkai, 1969.

Nosco, Peter, ed. *Confucianism and Tokugawa Culture*. Princeton: Princeton University Press, 1984.

Ogyū Sorai. *Master Sorai's Responsals: An Annotated Translation of "Sorai sensei tomonsho."* Translated by Samuel H. Yamashita. Honolulu: University of Hawaii Press, 1994.

———. *Ogyū Sorai's "Discourse on Government" (Seidan): An Annotated Transla-tion*. Translated by Olof Lidin. Wiesbaden: Harrassowitz Verlag, 1999.

———. *Ogyū Sorai's "Distinguishing the Way."* Translated by Olof Lidin. Tokyo: Sophia University Press, 1970.

———. *The Political Writings of Ogyū Sorai*. Translated by J. R. McEwan. Cam-bridge: Cambridge University Press, 1969.

Ooms, Herman. *Tokugawa Ideology: Early Constructs, 1570–1680*. Princeton: Princeton University Press, 1985.

———. *Tokugawa Village Practice: Class, Status, Power, Law*. Berkeley: University of California Press, 1996.

Passin, Herbert. *Society and Education in Japan*. New York: Teachers College Press, 1965.

Ro, Young-chan. *The Korean Neo-Confucianism of Yi Yulgok.* Albany: State University of New York Press, 1989.

Rozman, Gilbert. *Urban Networks in Ch'ing China and Tokugawa Japan.* Princeton: Princeton University Press, 1973.

Rubinger, Richard. *Private Academies of Tokugawa Japan.* Princeton: Princeton University Press, 1982.

Sadler, Arthur L. *The Maker of Modern Japan: The Life of Shogun Tokugawa Ieyasu.* 1932. Reprint, Rutland, Vt.: Tuttle, 1978.

Sansom, George. *A History of Japan.* Vol. 1, *To 1334.* Stanford, Calif.: Stanford University Press, 1958.

——. *A History of Japan.* Vol. 2, *1334–1615.* Stanford, Calif.: Stanford University Press, 1961.

——. *A History of Japan.* Vol. 3, *1615–1867.* Stanford, Calif.: Stanford University Press, 1963.

——. *The Western World and Japan.* London: Cresset Press, 1950.

Satow, Ernest. *The Jesuit Mission Press in Japan, 1591–1610.* London: Private printing, 1888.

Sawada, Janine. *Confucian Values and Popular Zen: Sekimon Shingaku in Eighteenth Century Japan.* Honolulu: University of Hawaii Press, 1993.

Sheldon, Charles D. *The Rise of the Merchant Class in Tokugawa Japan, 1600–1868.* Locust Valley, N.Y.: Augustin, 1958.

Sima Qian. *Records of the Historian: Chapters from the Shih Chi of Ssu-ma Ch'ien.* Translated by Burton Watson. New York: Columbia University Press, 1969.

Smith, Thomas. *The Agrarian Origins of Modern Japan.* Stanford, Calif.: Stanford University Press, 1959.

Smith, Warren W. *Confucianism in Modern Japan: A Study of Conservatism in Japanese Intellectual History.* Tokyo: Hokuseidō Press, 1959.

Sontoku Ninomiya. *A Peasant Sage of Japan: The Life and Work of Sontoku Ninomiya.* Translated by Tadasu Yoshimoto. New York: Longmans, Green, 1912. [Translation of *Hōtokuki*]

Soum, Jean-Francois. *Nakae Toju (1608–1648) et Kumazawa Banzan (1619–1691): Deux penseurs de l'époque d'Edo.* Paris: Institut des Hautes Études Japonaises/Centre d'Études Japonaises de l'INALCO, 2000.

Spae, Joseph. *Itō Jinsai: A Philosopher, Educator and Sinologist of the Tokugawa Period.* New York: Paragon, 1967.

Sugimoto, Masayoshi, and David L. Swain. *Science and Culture in Traditional Japan*, A.D. *600–1854*. Cambridge, Mass.: MIT Press, 1978.

Sugita Genpaku. *Dawn of Western Science in Japan: Rangaku Kotohajime*. Translated by Ryozo Matsumoto and Eiichi Kiyooka. Tokyo: Hokuseidō Press, 1969.

Takemura, Eiji. *The Perception of Work in Tokugawa Japan: A Study of Ishida Baigan and Ninomiya Sontoku*. Lanham, Md.: University Press of America, 1997.

Taylor, Rodney. *The Religious Dimensions of Confucianism*. Albany: State University of New York Press, 1990.

Toby, Ronald. *State and Diplomacy in Early Modern Japan: Asia in the Development of the Tokugawa Bakufu*. Princeton: Princeton University Press, 1984.

Totman, Conrad. *Early Modern Japan*. Berkeley: University of California Press, 1993.

———. *Politics in the Tokugawa Bakufu, 1600–1843*. Cambridge, Mass.: Harvard University Press, 1967.

———. *Tokugawa Ieyasu, Shogun: A Biography*. San Francisco: Heian, 1983.

Tsuda, Sōkichi. *An Inquiry into the Japanese Mind as Mirrored in Literature: The Flowering Period of Common People Literature*. Translated by Fukamatsu Matsuda. Tokyo: Japan Society for the Promotion of Science, 1970.

Tsukahira, Toshio. *Feudal Control in Tokugawa Japan: The Sankin Kōtai System*. Cambridge, Mass.: East Asian Research Center, Harvard University, 1966.

Tsunoda, Ryusaku, Wm. Theodore de Bary, and Donald Keene, eds. *Sources of Japanese Tradition*. New York: Columbia University Press, 1958.

Tu Weiming. *Centrality and Commonality: An Essay on Chung-yung*. Monographs of the Society for Asian and Comparative Philosophy, no. 3. Honolulu: University of Hawaii Press, 1976.

———. *Confucian Thought: Selfhood as Creative Transformation*. Albany: State University of New York Press, 1985.

Tu Weiming, and Mary Evelyn Tucker, eds. *Confucian Spirituality*. 2 vols. New York: Crossroad, 2003, 2004.

Tucker, John A. *Itō Jinsai's "Gōmo Jigi" and the Philosophical Definition of Early Modern Japan*. Leiden: Brill, 1998.

Tucker, Mary Evelyn. *Moral and Spiritual Cultivation in Japanese Neo-Confucianism: The Life and Thought of Kaibara Ekken, 1630–1714*. Albany: State University of New York Press, 1989.

Tucker, Mary Evelyn, and John Berthrong, eds. *Confucianism and Ecology: The Interrelation of Heaven, Earth, and Humans.* Cambridge, Mass.: Center for the Study of World Religions and Harvard University Press, 1998.

Vlastos, Stephen. *Peasant Protests and Uprisings in Tokugawa Japan.* Berkeley: University of California Press, 1986.

Wakabayashi, Bob Tadashi. *Anti-Foreignism and Western Learning in Early-Modern Japan.* Cambridge, Mass.: Harvard University Press, 1986.

Watson, William, ed. *The Great Japan Exhibition: Art of the Edo Period, 1600–1868.* London: Royal Academy of Art, 1981.

Webb, Herschel. *The Japanese Imperial Institution in the Tokugawa Period.* New York: Columbia University Press, 1968.

Yamamoto Tsunetomo. *Hagakure: The Book of the Samurai.* Translated by William Scott Wilson. Tokyo: Kodansha, 1979.

Yao, Xinzhong. *An Introduction to Confucianism.* Cambridge: Cambridge University Press, 2000.

Yazaki Takeo. *Social Change and the City in Japan, from Earliest Times Through the Industrial Revolution.* Tokyo: Japan Publications, 1968.

Yoshikawa Kojiro. *Jinsai, Sorai, Norinaga: Three Classical Philologists of Mid-Tokugawa Japan.* Tokyo: Tōhō gakkai, 1983.

Yuasa Yasuo. *The Body, Self-Cultivation, and Ki-Energy.* Translated by Shigenori Nagatomo and Monte S. Hull. Albany: State University of New York Press, 1993.

Zhu Xi. *Reflections on Things at Hand.* Translated by Wing-tsit Chan. New York: Columbia University Press, 1967.

Zhuangzi. *Chuang Tzu: Basic Writings.* Translated by Burton Watson. New York: Columbia University Press, 1996.

ARTICLES IN WESTERN LANGUAGES

Abe Yoshio. "The Characteristics of Japanese Confucianism." *Acta Asiatica* 25 (1973): 1–21.

——. "Development of Neo-Confucianism in Japan, Korea and China: A Comparative Study." *Acta Asiatica* 19 (1970): 16–39.

——. "Influence of Lo Ch'in-shun's *K'un-chih chi* in the Early Edo Period and the State of Practical Learning Among the Students of Kinoshita Jun'an and Yamazaki Ansai." Draft paper for the ACLS conference "Neo-

Confucianism and Practical Learning in the Ming and Early Tokugawa Periods," June 1974.

———. "The Unique Confucian Development of Japan: A Brief Survey and a Few Suggestions." *Asian Culture Quarterly* 4, no. 1 (1976): 8–13.

Backus, Robert L. "The Kansei Prohibition of Heterodoxy and Its Effects on Education." *Harvard Journal of Asiatic Studies* 39, no. 1 (1979): 55–106.

———. "The Motivation of Confucian Orthodoxy in Tokugawa Japan." *Harvard Journal of Asiatic Studies* 39, no. 2 (1979): 275–338.

———. "The Relation of Confucianism to the Tokugawa Bakufu as Revealed in the Kansei Educational Reform." *Harvard Journal of Asiatic Studies* 34 (1974): 97–162.

Bitō, Masahide. "Confucian Thought During the Tokugawa Period." In *Religion and the Family in East Asia*, edited by George A. De Vos and Takao Sofue, 127–138. Berkeley: University of California Press, 1986.

Bodart-Bailey, Beatrice. "The Confucian Scholar in Early Tokugawa Japan." In *État, société civile et sphère publique en Asie de l' Est*, edited by Charles Le Blanc and Alain Rocher, 191–208. Montreal: Université de Montréal, 1998.

———. "The Persecution of Confucianism in Early Tokugawa Japan." *Monumenta Nipponica* 48, no. 3 (1993): 293–314.

Boot, W. J. "The Adoption of Neo-Confucianism in Japan: The Role of Fujiwara Seika and Hayashi Razan." Ph.D. diss., University of Leiden, 1983.

Chan, Charles Wing-Hui. "The 'Benevolent Person' versus the 'Sage'": Ogyū Sorai's Critique of Chu Hsi." Ph.D. diss., University of Toronto, 1995.

Chan, Wing-tsit. "Chinese and Western Interpretations of *Jen* (Humanity)." *Journal of Chinese Philosophy* 2 (1975): 107–129.

———. "The Evolution of the Confucian Concept *Jen*." *Philosophy East and West* 4 (1955): 295–319.

———. "The Evolution of the Neo-Confucian Concept of *Li* as Principle." *Tsing Hua Journal of Chinese Studies* 5, no. 2 (1964): 132–149

Ching, Julia. "The Idea of God in Nakae Tōju." *Japanese Journal of Religious Studies* 11, no. 4 (1984): 293–312.

Craig, Albert M. "Science and Confucianism in Tokugawa Japan." In *Changing Japanese Attitudes Toward Modernization*, edited by Marius Jansen, 133–166. Princeton: Princeton University Press, 1965.

Dilworth, David A. "*Jitsugaku* as an Ontological Conception: Continuities and Discontinuities in Early and Mid-Tokugawa Thought." In *Principle and*

Practicality: Essays in Neo-Confucianim and Practical Learning, edited by Wm. Theodore de Bary and Irene Bloom, 471–514. New York: Columbia University Press, 1979.

Dore, Ronald P. "The Legacy of Tokugawa Education." In *Changing Japanese Attitudes Toward Modernization*, edited by Marius Jansen, 99–131. Princeton: Princeton University Press, 1965.

Gedalecia, David. "Excursion into Substance and Function: The Development of the *T'i-Yung* Paradigm in Chu Hsi." *Philosophy East and West* 24, no. 4 (1974): 444–451.

Griggs, Martin Pierce, trans. "Record of Grave Doubts" [part 1]. In *Readings in Tokugawa Thought*, 2nd ed., edited by Tetsuo Najita, 69–97. Chicago: Center for East Asian Studies, University of Chicago, 1994.

Hall, John W. "The Confucian Teacher in Tokugawa Japan." In *Confucianism in Action*, edited by David Nivison and Arthur Wright, 268–301. Stanford, Calif.: Stanford University Press, 1959.

Harootunian, Harry D. "The Functions of China in Tokugawa Thought." In *The Chinese and the Japanese*, edited by Akira Iriye, 9–36. Princeton: Princeton University Press, 1980.

Hatton, Russel. "*Chi's* Role Within the Psychology of Chu Hsi." *Journal of Chinese Philosophy* 9, no. 4 (1932): 441–469.

Henderson, John B. "Strategies in Neo-Confucian Heresiography." In *Imagining Boundaries: Changing Confucian Doctrines, Texts, and Hermeneutics*, edited by Kai-wing Chow, On-cho Ng, and John B. Henderson, 107–120. Albany: State University of New York Press, 1999.

Huang, Siu-chi. "Chang Tsai's Concept of *Ch'i*." *Philosophy East and West* 18, no. 4 (1968): 247–259.

Kang, Thomas. "The Making of Confucian Societies in Tokugawa Japan and Yi Korea." Ph.D. diss., American University, 1971.

Keene, Donald. "Characteristic Responses to Confucianism in Tokugawa Literature." In *Confucianism in Tokugawa Culture*, edited by Peter Nosco, 120–137. Princeton: Princeton University Press, 1984.

Knox, George W. "Ki, Ri, and Ten." *Asiatic Sociey of Japan* 20, no. 12 (1872–1873): 171–177.

Kristiansen, Roald. "Western Science and Japanese Neo-Confucianism: A History of Their Interaction and Transformation." *Japanese Religions* 21 (1996): 253–282.

Marti, Jeffrey. "Intellectual and Moral Foundations of Empirical Agronomy in Eighteenth-Century Japan." In *Select Papers from the Center for Far Eastern Studies, University of Chicago*, vol. 2. Chicago: Center for Far Eastern Studies, University of Chicago, 1978.

McMullen, Ian James. "Itō Jinsai and the Meaning of Words." *Monumenta Nipponica* 54 (1999): 509–520.

Mercer, Rosemary. "Picturing the Universe: Adventures with Miura Baien at the Borderland of Philosophy and Science." *Philosophy East and West* 48, no. 3 (1998): 478–502.

Minamoto Ryōen. "The Development of the *Jitsugaku* Concept in the Tokugawa Period." *Philosophical Studies of Japan* 11 (1975): 61–93.

Najita, Tetsuo. "Intellectual Change in Early Eighteenth-Century Tokugawa Confucianism." *Journal of Asian Studies* 34, no. 4 (1975): 931–944.

Nakai, Kate Wildman. "The Naturalization of Confucianism in Tokugawa Japan: The Problem of Sinocentrism." *Harvard Journal of Asian Studies* 40 (1980): 157–199.

Ng, On-cho, and Kai-wing Chow. "Introduction: Fluidity of the Confucian Canon and Discursive Strategies." In *Imagining Boundaries: Changing Confucian Doctrines, Texts, and Hermeneutics*, edited by Kai-wing Chow, On-cho Ng, and John B. Henderson, 1–15. Albany: State University of New York Press, 1999.

Nosco, Peter, "The Religious Dimension of Confucianism in Japan: Introduction." *Philosophy East and West* 48, no. 1 (1998): 1–4.

Okada Takehiko. "The Chu Hsi and Wang Yang-ming Schools at the End of the Ming and Tokugawa Periods." *Philosophy East and West* 23, nos. 1–2 (1973): 139–162.

——. "Practical Learning in the Chu Hsi School: Yamazaki Ansai and Kaibara Ekken." In *Principle and Practicality: Essays in Neo-Confucianim and Practical Learning*, edited by Wm. Theodore de Bary and Irene Bloom, 231–305. New York: Columbia University Press, 1979.

Sakai Atsuharu. "Kaibara Ekiken and *Onna-Daigaku*." *Cultural Nippon* 7, no. 4 (1939): 43–56.

Steben, Barry. "Nakae Tōju and the Birth of Wang Yang-Ming Learning in Japan." *Monumenta Serica* 46 (1998): 233–263.

Tang, Chün-I. "Chang Tsai's Theory of Mind and Its Metaphysical Basis." *Philosophy East and West* 6, no. 2 (1956): 113–136.

Tu Weiming. "The Continuity of Being: Chinese Visions of Nature." In *Nature in Asian Traditions of Thought*, edited by J. Baird Callicott and Roger Ames, 67–78. Albany: State University of New York Press, 1989.

——."The Creative Tension Between *Jen* and *Li*." *Philosophy East and West* 18, nos. 1–2 (1968): 29–39.

——. "*Li* as a Process of Humanization." *Philosophy East and West* 22, no. 2 (1972): 187–201.

——. "The 'Moral Universal' from the Perspectives of East Asian Thought." *Philosophy East and West* 31, no. 3 (1981): 259–267.

——. "The Neo-Confucian Concept of Man." *Philosophy East and West* 21, no. 1 (1971): 79–87.

——. "On Neo-Confucianism and Human Relatedness." In *Religion and the Family*, edited by George A. De Vos and Takao Sofue, 111–125. Berkeley: University of California Press, 1986.

Tucker, Mary Evelyn. "The Adaptation of Confucianism in Japan." In *Confucian Spirituality*, edited by Tu Weiming and Mary Evelyn Tucker, 2:247–269. New York: Crossroad, 2004.

——. "Confucian Cosmology and Ecological Ethics: *Qi, Li* and the Role of the Human." In *Ethics in the World Religions*, edited by Joseph Runzo and Nancy Martin, 331–345. Oxford: Oneworld, 2001.

——. "Confucian Education in Tokugawa Japan: The Case of the Shizutani School in Okayama Prefecture." In *État, société civile et sphère publique en Asie de l'Est*, edited by Charles Le Blanc and Alain Rocher, 157–189. Montreal: Université de Montréal, 1998.

——. "Confucian Ethics and Cosmology for a Sustainable Future." In *When Worlds Converge: What Science and Religion Tell Us About the Story of the Universe and Our Place in It*, edited by Clifford N. Matthews, Mary Evelyn Tucker, and Philip Hefner, 310–323. Chicago: Open Court, 2002.

——. "Confucianism in Japan." In *Encyclopedia of Chinese Philosophy*, edited by Antonio Cua, 97–102. New York: Routledge, 2003.

——. "Cosmology, Science, and Ethics in Japanese Neo-Confucianism." In *Science and Religion in Search of Cosmic Purpose*, edited by John F. Haught, 69–90. Washington, D.C.: Georgetown University Press, 2000.

——. "Humaneness as Personal and Cosmic." In *Jen Agape Tao with Tu Weiming*, edited by Marko Zlomislic and David Goicoechea, 50–70. New York: Global Scholarly Publications, 1999.

——. "Introduction." In *Confucian Spirituality*, edited by Tu Weiming and Mary Evelyn Tucker, 2:1–35. New York: Crossroad, 2004.

——. "Kaibara Ekken: His Life and Thought" [in Chinese]. In *Proceedings from the International Conference on Traditional Culture in East Asia, 1996. Studies on East Asian Cultures: Development of Traditional Culture*, edited by Huang Chun-chieh. Taipei: Zhengzhong shuju, 1996. ["Kaibara Ekken zhi shengtai zhexue yu daode guan." In *Dongya wenhua de tanso: Chuantong wenhua de fazhang*]

——. "Kaibara Ekken's *Precepts on the Family*." In *An Anthology of Asian Religions in Practice*, edited by Donald S. Lopez Jr., 613–628. Princeton: Princeton University Press, 2002. [First published in *Religions of Japan in Practice*, edited by George J. Tanabe Jr., 38–52. Princeton: Princeton University Press, 1999]

——. "The Philosophy of *Ch'i* as an Ecological Cosmology." In *Confucianism and Ecology: The Interrelation of Heaven, Earth, and Humans*, edited by Mary Evelyn Tucker and John Berthrong, 186–207. Cambridge, Mass.: Center for the Study of World Religions and Harvard University Press, 1998.

——. "The Potential of Confucian Values for Environmental Ethics." In *Proceedings of the Environmental Security Conference on Cultural Attitudes About the Environment and Ecology, and Their Connection to Regional Political Stability*, edited by K. Mark Leek, 133–142. Columbus, Ohio: Battelle Press, 1999.

——. "Religious Dimensions of Confucianism: Cosmology and Cultivation." *Philosophy East and West* 48, no. 1 (1998): 5–45.

——. "A View of Philanthropy in Japan: Confucian Ethics and Education." In *Philanthropy in the World's Traditions*, edited by Warren F. Ilchman, Stanley N. Katz, and Edward L. Queen II, 169–193. Bloomington: Indiana University Press, 1998.

——. "Working Toward a Shared Global Ethic: Confucian Perspectives." In *Toward a Global Civilization? The Contribution of Religions*, edited by Patricia M. Mische and Melissa Merkling, 177–193. New York: Lang, 2001.

——, trans. "Kaibara Ekken: Human Nature and the Study of Nature." In *Sources of Japanese Tradition*, edited by Wm. Theodore de Bary, Carol Gluck, and Arthur E. Tiedemann, 2:105–114. New York: Columbia University Press, 2005. [Introduction and selected translations from Kaibara Ekken's *Record of Great Doubts* and *Elementary Learning for Children*]

Tucker, Mary Evelyn, and John Berthrong. "Introduction." In *Confucianism and Ecology: The Interrelation of Heaven, Earth, and Humans*, edited by Mary Evelyn Tucker and John Berthrong, xxxv–xlv. Cambridge, Mass.: Center for the Study of World Religions and Harvard University Press, 1998.

Yamanoi, Yu. "The Great Ultimate and Heaven in Chu Hsi's Philosophy." In *Chu Hsi and Neo-Confucianism*, edited by Wing-tsit Chan, 79–115. Honolulu: University of Hawaii Press: 1986.

142; and Ekken, 26, 70n.43;
Knowledge Painfully Acquired, 21, 142,
154n.55; on material force, 14, 20–25,
35, 113; on metaphysics, 22–23; on
principle, 22, 23, 24, 35, 91–92, 113

Maruyama Masao, 50, 56–57
material force (*ch'i; ki; qi*): and Ancient
Learning, 32; and Buddhism, 15, 143,
148; cosmology of, 41–48; and death,
142; Ekken on, 24–25, 26, 60, 64–67;
and Heaven and Earth, 123–127; and
human nature, 46, 47, 89, 104–105;
and humaneness, 18, 19, 132–133;
interpretations of, 55–58, 59, 95, 112;
Luo Qinshun on, 14, 20–25, 35, 113;
monism of, 4, 5, 19, 20–25, 48, 50, 60,
65, 88–89, 102–103, 144–149; and
physical form, 131–132; and practical
learning, 48–55; and principle, 4, 5, 13,
14, 21, 26, 31, 34, 35, 40–48, 59, 65, 83,
88–89, 102–103, 105, 106, 112, 124,
143–149, 152n.37; school of (*kigaku*),
56; and self-cultivation, 14, 20, 65; and
Supreme Ultimate, 44, 45, 127, 143,
144–149; and transformation, 14–20,
67; and vitalism, 59–60; and yin and
yang, 46, 88, 143, 144–149; Zhang Zai
on, 14–20
mathematics, 5, 51
Mean. See *Doctrine of the Mean*
medicine, 5, 51, 71n.57
meditation, 11, 38, 83
Mencius, 9, 59, 65, 95, 118, 138; and
Ancient Learning, 30, 32; on human
nature, 90, 103, 105, 158n.110; on
learning, 37–38, 100, 101, 102, 140;
on material force, 13, 66; *Mencius*, 10,
100, 132; vs. Song Confucians, 83, 98,
99, 105, 106, 112, 113, 114–117; and
transmission of the Way, 81, 82, 84,
85, 97; and Zhang Zai, 1
merchants, 29, 30, 51

metaphysics, 11, 41, 48, 56, 57; Luo
Qinshun on, 22–23; vs. physical form,
122–127
Minamoto Ryōen, 49, 56, 57
mind-and-heart (*kokoro; shin; xin*), 12, 83,
95, 103, 140; and material force, 15,
20, 66; and nature, 21, 24; and
reverence, 136, 137–144, 142
Ming Confucianism, 39, 96, 109–110, 113
missionaries, 27
Miyazaki Yasusada, *Nōgyō zensho*, 5
modernity, 49–50, 55–56
monism: of Heaven and Earth and
physical nature, 102–106; of material
force and principle, 4, 5, 19, 20–25,
48, 50, 60, 65, 88–89, 102–103, 144–
149; vs. Zhu Xi, 21, 40–41, 42, 89,
149, 153nn.38,39, 156n.84, 157n.94
moral treatises (*kunmono*), 4, 37
morality, 22, 26, 46, 49, 56, 118, 137;
Confucian, 9–10, 29–30; and
cosmology, 11–12, 18–20; and
dualism, 48; and holism, 60, 61; and
material force, 18, 20; of Song
Confucians, 84, 106, 109–110, 112
Mori Rantaku, 32
Mu Bozhang, 129, 130, 161n.164

Nagasaki, 2, 27, 51
Najita, Tetsuo, 29, 30, 57
Nakae Tōju, 30, 57
naturalism, 40–41, 58; vitalistic, 4, 5, 26,
45–46
nature, 56–60; Ekken on, 5, 24, 40–41,
42; filiality toward, 67; gratitude to,
47–48; and human beings, 61, 64, 65;
and human mind, 21, 24; and material
force, 4, 14, 20, 47, 64–67; and
practical learning, 32, 51, 55; reverence
for, 57, 64; Song Confucians on, 112;
Zhu Xi on, 32, 40–41, 42
Neo-Confucianism: adaptability of, 49;
cosmology of, 40–41, 59; and dissent,

Translations from the Asian Classics

Major Plays of Chikamatsu, tr. Donald Keene 1961

Four Major Plays of Chikamatsu, tr. Donald Keene. Paperback ed. only. 1961; rev. ed. 1997

Records of the Grand Historian of China, translated from the Shih chi of Ssu-ma Ch'ien, tr. Burton Watson, 2 vols. 1961

Instructions for Practical Living and Other Neo-Confucian Writings by Wang Yang-ming, tr. Wing-tsit Chan 1963

Hsün Tzu: Basic Writings, tr. Burton Watson, paperback ed. only. 1963; rev. ed. 1996

Chuang Tzu: Basic Writings, tr. Burton Watson, paperback ed. only. 1964; rev. ed. 1996

The Mahābhārata, tr. Chakravarthi V. Narasimhan. Also in paperback ed. 1965; rev. ed. 1997

The Manyōshū, Nippon Gakujutsu Shinkōkai edition 1965

Su Tung-p'o: Selections from a Sung Dynasty Poet, tr. Burton Watson. Also in paperback ed. 1965

Bhartrihari: Poems, tr. Barbara Stoler Miller. Also in paperback ed. 1967

Basic Writings of Mo Tzu, Hsün Tzu, and Han Fei Tzu, tr. Burton Watson. Also in separate paperback eds. 1967

The Awakening of Faith, Attributed to Aśvaghosha, tr. Yoshito S. Hakeda. Also in paperback ed. 1967

Reflections on Things at Hand: The Neo-Confucian Anthology, comp. Chu Hsi and Lü Tsu-ch'ien, tr. Wing-tsit Chan 1967

The Platform Sutra of the Sixth Patriarch, tr. Philip B. Yampolsky. Also in paperback ed. 1967

Essays in Idleness: The Tsurezuregusa of Kenkō, tr. Donald Keene. Also in paperback ed. 1967

The Pillow Book of Sei Shōnagon, tr. Ivan Morris, 2 vols. 1967

Two Plays of Ancient India: The Little Clay Cart and the Minister's Seal, tr. J. A. B. van Buitenen 1968

The Complete Works of Chuang Tzu, tr. Burton Watson 1968

The Romance of the Western Chamber (Hsi Hsiang chi), tr. S. I. Hsiung. Also in paperback ed. 1968

The Manyōshū, Nippon Gakujutsu Shinkōkai edition. Paperback ed. only. 1969

Records of the Historian: Chapters from the Shih chi of Ssu-ma Ch'ien, tr. Burton Watson. Paperback ed. only. 1969

Cold Mountain: 100 Poems by the T'ang Poet Han-shan, tr. Burton Watson. Also in paperback ed. 1970

Twenty Plays of the Nō Theatre, ed. Donald Keene. Also in paperback ed. 1970

Chūshingura: The Treasury of Loyal Retainers, tr. Donald Keene. Also in paperback ed. 1971; rev. ed. 1997

The Zen Master Hakuin: Selected Writings, tr. Philip B. Yampolsky 1971

Chinese Rhyme-Prose: Poems in the Fu Form from the Han and Six Dynasties Periods, tr. Burton Watson. Also in paperback ed. 1971

Kūkai: Major Works, tr. Yoshito S. Hakeda. Also in paperback ed. 1972

The Old Man Who Does as He Pleases: Selections from the Poetry and Prose of Lu Yu, tr. Burton Watson 1973

The Lion's Roar of Queen Śrīmālā, tr. Alex and Hideko Wayman 1974

Courtier and Commoner in Ancient China: Selections from the History of the Former Han by Pan Ku, tr. Burton Watson. Also in paperback ed. 1974

Japanese Literature in Chinese, vol. 1: *Poetry and Prose in Chinese by Japanese Writers of the Early Period*, tr. Burton Watson 1975

Japanese Literature in Chinese, vol. 2: *Poetry and Prose in Chinese by Japanese Writers of the Later Period*, tr. Burton Watson 1976

Scripture of the Lotus Blossom of the Fine Dharma, tr. Leon Hurvitz. Also in paperback ed. 1976

Love Song of the Dark Lord: Jayadeva's Gītagovinda, tr. Barbara Stoler Miller. Also in paperback ed. Cloth ed. includes critical text of the Sanskrit. 1977; rev. ed. 1997

Ryōkan: Zen Monk-Poet of Japan, tr. Burton Watson 1977

Calming the Mind and Discerning the Real: From the Lam rim chen mo of Tson-kha-pa, tr. Alex Wayman 1978

The Hermit and the Love-Thief: Sanskrit Poems of Bhartrihari and Bilhaṇa, tr. Barbara Stoler Miller 1978

The Lute: Kao Ming's P'i-p'a chi, tr. Jean Mulligan. Also in paperback ed. 1980

A Chronicle of Gods and Sovereigns: Jinnō Shōtōki of Kitabatake Chikafusa, tr. H. Paul Varley 1980

Among the Flowers: The Hua-chien chi, tr. Lois Fusek 1982

Grass Hill: Poems and Prose by the Japanese Monk Gensei, tr. Burton Watson 1983

Doctors, Diviners, and Magicians of Ancient China: Biographies of Fang-shih, tr. Kenneth J. DeWoskin. Also in paperback ed. 1983

Theater of Memory: The Plays of Kālidāsa, ed. Barbara Stoler Miller. Also in paperback ed. 1984

The Columbia Book of Chinese Poetry: From Early Times to the Thirteenth Century, ed. and tr. Burton Watson. Also in paperback ed. 1984

Poems of Love and War: From the Eight Anthologies and the Ten Long Poems of Classical Tamil, tr. A. K. Ramanujan. Also in paperback ed. 1985

The Bhagavad Gita: Krishna's Counsel in Time of War, tr. Barbara Stoler Miller 1986

The Columbia Book of Later Chinese Poetry, ed. and tr. Jonathan Chaves. Also in paperback ed. 1986

The Tso Chuan: Selections from China's Oldest Narrative History, tr. Burton Watson 1989

Waiting for the Wind: Thirty-six Poets of Japan's Late Medieval Age, tr. Steven Carter 1989

Selected Writings of Nichiren, ed. Philip B. Yampolsky 1990

Saigyō, Poems of a Mountain Home, tr. Burton Watson 1990

The Book of Lieh Tzu: A Classic of the Tao, tr. A. C. Graham. Morningside ed. 1990

The Tale of an Anklet: An Epic of South India—The Cilappatikāram of Iḷaṅkō Aṭikaḷ, tr. R. Parthasarathy 1993

Waiting for the Dawn: A Plan for the Prince, tr. with introduction by Wm. Theodore de Bary 1993

Yoshitsune and the Thousand Cherry Trees: A Masterpiece of the Eighteenth-Century Japanese Puppet Theater, tr., annotated, and with introduction by Stanleigh H. Jones, Jr. 1993

The Lotus Sutra, tr. Burton Watson. Also in paperback ed. 1993

The Classic of Changes: A New Translation of the I Ching as Interpreted by Wang Bi, tr. Richard John Lynn 1994

Beyond Spring: Tz'u Poems of the Sung Dynasty, tr. Julie Landau 1994

The Columbia Anthology of Traditional Chinese Literature, ed. Victor H. Mair 1994

Scenes for Mandarins: The Elite Theater of the Ming, tr. Cyril Birch 1995

Letters of Nichiren, ed. Philip B. Yampolsky; tr. Burton Watson et al. 1996

Unforgotten Dreams: Poems by the Zen Monk Shōtetsu, tr. Steven D. Carter 1997

The Vimalakirti Sutra, tr. Burton Watson 1997

Japanese and Chinese Poems to Sing: The Wakan rōei shū, tr. J. Thomas Rimer and Jonathan Chaves 1997

Breeze Through Bamboo: Kanshi of Ema Saikō, tr. Hiroaki Sato 1998

A Tower for the Summer Heat, by Li Yu, tr. Patrick Hanan 1998

Traditional Japanese Theater: An Anthology of Plays, by Karen Brazell 1998

The Original Analects: Sayings of Confucius and His Successors (0479–0249), by E. Bruce Brooks and A. Taeko Brooks 1998

The Classic of the Way and Virtue: A New Translation of the Tao-te ching *of Laozi as Interpreted by Wang Bi,* tr. Richard John Lynn 1999

The Four Hundred Songs of War and Wisdom: An Anthology of Poems from Classical Tamil, *The* Puṟanāṉūṟu, ed. and tr. George L. Hart and Hank Heifetz 1999

Original Tao: Inward Training (Nei-yeh) *and the Foundations of Taoist Mysticism,* by Harold D. Roth 1999

Lao Tzu's Tao Te Ching: *A Translation of the Startling New Documents Found at Guodian,* by Robert G. Henricks 2000

The Shorter Columbia Anthology of Traditional Chinese Literature, ed. Victor H. Mair 2000

Mistress and Maid (Jiaohongji), by Meng Chengshun, tr. Cyril Birch 2001

Chikamatsu: Five Late Plays, tr. and ed. C. Andrew Gerstle 2001

The Essential Lotus: Selections from the Lotus Sutra, tr. Burton Watson 2002

Early Modern Japanese Literature: An Anthology, 1600–1900, ed. Haruo Shirane 2002

The Sound of the Kiss, or The Story That Must Never Be Told: Pingali Suranna's Kalapurnodayamu, tr. Vecheru Narayana Rao and David Shulman 2003

The Selected Poems of Du Fu, tr. Burton Watson 2003

Far Beyond the Field: Haiku by Japanese Women, tr. Makoto Ueda 2003

Just Living: Poems and Prose by the Japanese Monk Tonna, ed. and tr. Steven D. Carter 2003

Han Feizi: Basic Writings, tr. Burton Watson 2003

Mozi: Basic Writings, tr. Burton Watson 2003

Xunzi: Basic Writings, tr. Burton Watson 2003

Zhuangzi: Basic Writings, tr. Burton Watson 2003

The Awakening of Faith, Attributed to Aśvaghosha, tr. Yoshito S. Hakeda, introduction by Ryuichi Abe 2005

The Tales of the Heike, tr. Burton Watson, ed. Haruo Shirane 2006

Tales of Moonlight and Rain, by Ueda Akinari, tr. with introduction by Anthony H. Chambers 2007

Traditional Japanese Literature: An Anthology, Beginnings to 1600, ed. Haruo Shirane 2007

Modern Asian Literature

Modern Japanese Drama: An Anthology, ed. and tr. Ted. Takaya. Also in paperback ed. 1979

Mask and Sword: Two Plays for the Contemporary Japanese Theater, by Yamazaki Masakazu, tr. J. Thomas Rimer 1980

Yokomitsu Riichi, Modernist, by Dennis Keene 1980

Nepali Visions, Nepali Dreams: The Poetry of Laxmiprasad Devkota, tr. David Rubin 1980

Literature of the Hundred Flowers, vol. 1: Criticism and Polemics, ed. Hualing Nieh 1981

Literature of the Hundred Flowers, vol. 2: Poetry and Fiction, ed. Hualing Nieh 1981

Modern Chinese Stories and Novellas, 1919–1949, ed. Joseph S. M. Lau, C. T. Hsia, and Leo Ou-fan Lee. Also in paperback ed. 1984
A View by the Sea, by Yasuoka Shōtarō, tr. Kären Wigen Lewis 1984
Other Worlds: Arishima Takeo and the Bounds of Modern Japanese Fiction, by Paul Anderer 1984
Selected Poems of Sŏ Chŏngju, tr. with introduction by David R. McCann 1989
The Sting of Life: Four Contemporary Japanese Novelists, by Van C. Gessel 1989
Stories of Osaka Life, by Oda Sakunosuke, tr. Burton Watson 1990
The Bodhisattva, or Samantabhadra, by Ishikawa Jun, tr. with introduction by William Jefferson Tyler 1990
The Travels of Lao Ts'an, by Liu T'ieh-yün, tr. Harold Shadick. Morningside ed. 1990
Three Plays by Kōbō Abe, tr. with introduction by Donald Keene 1993
The Columbia Anthology of Modern Chinese Literature, ed. Joseph S. M. Lau and Howard Goldblatt 1995
Modern Japanese Tanka, ed. and tr. Makoto Ueda 1996
Masaoka Shiki: Selected Poems, ed. and tr. Burton Watson 1997
Writing Women in Modern China: An Anthology of Women's Literature from the Early Twentieth Century, ed. and tr. Amy D. Dooling and Kristina M. Torgeson 1998
American Stories, by Nagai Kafū, tr. Mitsuko Iriye 2000
The Paper Door and Other Stories, by Shiga Naoya, tr. Lane Dunlop 2001
Grass for My Pillow, by Saiichi Maruya, tr. Dennis Keene 2002
For All My Walking: Free-Verse Haiku of Taneda Santōka, with Excerpts from His Diaries, tr. Burton Watson 2003
The Columbia Anthology of Modern Japanese Literature, vol. 1: *From Restoration to Occupation, 1868–1945*, ed. J. Thomas Rimer and Van C. Gessel 2005
The Columbia Anthology of Modern Japanese Literature, vol. 2: *From 1945 to the Present*, ed. J. Thomas Rimer and Van C. Gessel 2007

Studies in Asian Culture

The Ōnin War: History of Its Origins and Background, with a Selective Translation of the Chronicle of Ōnin, by H. Paul Varley 1967
Chinese Government in Ming Times: Seven Studies, ed. Charles O. Hucker 1969
The Actors' Analects (Yakusha Rongo), ed. and tr. Charles J. Dunn and Bungō Torigoe 1969
Self and Society in Ming Thought, by Wm. Theodore de Bary and the Conference on Ming Thought. Also in paperback ed. 1970
A History of Islamic Philosophy, by Majid Fakhry, 2d ed. 1983
Phantasies of a Love Thief: The Caurapañcāśikā Attributed to Bilhaṇa, by Barbara Stoler Miller 1971
Iqbal: Poet-Philosopher of Pakistan, ed. Hafeez Malik 1971
The Golden Tradition: An Anthology of Urdu Poetry, ed. and tr. Ahmed Ali. Also in paperback ed. 1973

Conquerors and Confucians: Aspects of Political Change in Late Yüan China, by John W. Dardess 1973

The Unfolding of Neo-Confucianism, by Wm. Theodore de Bary and the Conference on Seventeenth-Century Chinese Thought. Also in paperback ed. 1975

To Acquire Wisdom: The Way of Wang Yang-ming, by Julia Ching 1976

Gods, Priests, and Warriors: The Bhru.gus of the Mahābhārata, by Robert P. Goldman 1977

Mei Yao-ch'en and the Development of Early Sung Poetry, by Jonathan Chaves 1976

The Legend of Semimaru, Blind Musician of Japan, by Susan Matisoff 1977

Sir Sayyid Ahmad Khan and Muslim Modernization in India and Pakistan, by Hafeez Malik 1980

The Khilafat Movement: Religious Symbolism and Political Mobilization in India, by Gail Minault 1982

The World of K'ung Shang-jen: A Man of Letters in Early Ch'ing China, by Richard Strassberg 1983

The Lotus Boat: The Origins of Chinese Tz'u Poetry in T'ang Popular Culture, by Marsha L. Wagner 1984

Expressions of Self in Chinese Literature, ed. Robert E. Hegel and Richard C. Hessney 1985

Songs for the Bride: Women's Voices and Wedding Rites of Rural India, by W. G. Archer; ed. Barbara Stoler Miller and Mildred Archer 1986

The Confucian Kingship in Korea: Yo and the Politics of Sagacity, by JaHyun Kim Haboush 1988

Companions to Asian Studies

Approaches to the Oriental Classics, ed. Wm. Theodore de Bary 1959

Early Chinese Literature, by Burton Watson. Also in paperback ed. 1962

Approaches to Asian Civilizations, ed. Wm. Theodore de Bary and Ainslie T. Embree 1964

The Classic Chinese Novel: A Critical Introduction, by C. T. Hsia. Also in paperback ed. 1968

Chinese Lyricism: Shih Poetry from the Second to the Twelfth Century, tr. Burton Watson. Also in paperback ed. 1971

A Syllabus of Indian Civilization, by Leonard A. Gordon and Barbara Stoler Miller 1971

Twentieth-Century Chinese Stories, ed. C. T. Hsia and Joseph S. M. Lau. Also in paperback ed. 1971

A Syllabus of Chinese Civilization, by J. Mason Gentzler, 2d ed. 1972

A Syllabus of Japanese Civilization, by H. Paul Varley, 2d ed. 1972

An Introduction to Chinese Civilization, ed. John Meskill, with the assistance of J. Mason Gentzler 1973

An Introduction to Japanese Civilization, ed. Arthur E. Tiedemann 1974

Ukifune: Love in the Tale of Genji, ed. Andrew Pekarik 1982
The Pleasures of Japanese Literature, by Donald Keene 1988
A Guide to Oriental Classics, ed. Wm. Theodore de Bary and Ainslie T. Embree; 3d edition ed. Amy Vladeck Heinrich, 2 vols. 1989

Introduction to Asian Civilizations
Wm. Theodore de Bary, General Editor

Sources of Japanese Tradition, 1958; paperback ed., 2 vols., 1964. 2d ed., vol. 1, 2001, compiled by Wm. Theodore de Bary, Donald Keene, George Tanabe, and Paul Varley; vol. 2, 2005, compiled by Wm. Theodore de Bary, Carol Gluck, and Arthur E. Tiedemann; vol. 2, abridged, 2 pts., 2006, compiled by Wm. Theodore de Bary, Carol Gluck, and Arthur E. Tiedemann
Sources of Indian Tradition, 1958; paperback ed., 2 vols., 1964. 2d ed., 2 vols., 1988
Sources of Chinese Tradition, 1960, paperback ed., 2 vols., 1964. 2d ed., vol. 1, 1999, compiled by Wm. Theodore de Bary and Irene Bloom; vol. 2, 2000, compiled by Wm. Theodore de Bary and Richard Lufrano
Sources of Korean Tradition, 1997; 2 vols., vol. 1, 1997, compiled by Peter H. Lee and Wm. Theodore de Bary; vol. 2, 2001, compiled by Yŏngho Ch'oe, Peter H. Lee, and Wm. Theodore de Bary

Neo-Confucian Studies

Instructions for Practical Living and Other Neo-Confucian Writings by Wang Yang-ming, tr. Wing-tsit Chan 1963
Reflections on Things at Hand: The Neo-Confucian Anthology, comp. Chu Hsi and Lü Tsu-ch'ien, tr. Wing-tsit Chan 1967
Self and Society in Ming Thought, by Wm. Theodore de Bary and the Conference on Ming Thought. Also in paperback ed. 1970
The Unfolding of Neo-Confucianism, by Wm. Theodore de Bary and the Conference on Seventeenth-Century Chinese Thought. Also in paperback ed. 1975
Principle and Practicality: Essays in Neo-Confucianism and Practical Learning, ed. Wm. Theodore de Bary and Irene Bloom. Also in paperback ed. 1979
The Syncretic Religion of Lin Chao-en, by Judith A. Berling 1980
The Renewal of Buddhism in China: Chu-hung and the Late Ming Synthesis, by Chün-fang Yü 1981
Neo-Confucian Orthodoxy and the Learning of the Mind-and-Heart, by Wm. Theodore de Bary 1981
Yüan Thought: Chinese Thought and Religion Under the Mongols, ed. Hok-lam Chan and Wm. Theodore de Bary 1982
The Liberal Tradition in China, by Wm. Theodore de Bary 1983
The Development and Decline of Chinese Cosmology, by John B. Henderson 1984

The Rise of Neo-Confucianism in Korea, by Wm. Theodore de Bary and JaHyun Kim Haboush 1985

Chiao Hung and the Restructuring of Neo-Confucianism in Late Ming, by Edward T. Ch'ien 1985

Neo-Confucian Terms Explained: Pei-hsi tzu-i, by Ch'en Ch'un, ed. and tr. Wing-tsit Chan 1986

Knowledge Painfully Acquired: K'un-chih chi, by Lo Ch'in-shun, ed. and tr. Irene Bloom 1987

To Become a Sage: The Ten Diagrams on Sage Learning, by Yi T'oegye, ed. and tr. Michael C. Kalton 1988

The Message of the Mind in Neo-Confucian Thought, by Wm. Theodore de Bary 1989

The Columbia Anthology of Modern Chinese Literature, 2d ed., ed. Joseph S. M. Lau and Howard Goldblatt